908   1ST   10
                                             T-

THE RED SNOW

By James Greiner

WAGER WITH THE WIND
THE RED SNOW

THE RED SNOW

by
James Greiner

Foreword by
Margaret E. Murie

Doubleday & Company, Inc.
Garden City, New York
1980

All of the characters
in this book are fictitious,
and any resemblance to actual persons,
living or dead,
is purely coincidental.

BOOK DESIGN BY BENTE HAMANN

ISBN: 0-385-13169-0
Library of Congress Catalog Card Number: 77-82943

First Edition

ACKNOWLEDGMENTS

The writing of a factual book which deals with the intricacies that define the life history of any wild species must be the result not only of the author's own efforts but those of many others. Their assistance takes a variety of forms which range from simple encouragement and criticism to the direct inclusion of their own expertise in the exhaustive task of producing an entirely factual book.

It is impossible to single out everyone who has taken part in the writing of *The Red Snow*, and to those who are not mentioned here by name, I extend my sincere thanks for their part in the story of the St. George Creek wolves.

I owe a debt of gratitude to Mr. Robert Stephenson, Biologist for Wolf Studies with the Alaska Department of Fish and Game. During the writing he offered encouragement when I needed it most. Bob Stephenson's qualifications to judge the validity of the story stem from many years of personal observation of wolves, a decade devoted to radio collar or telimetry research, along with the coordination of the department's Eskimo/Wolf Programs.

Dr. Victor Vanballenberghe is also employed by the Alaska Department of Fish and Game as Statewide Fur Bearer Biologist. A wildlife ecologist who conducted extensive wolf research with L. David Mech in Minnesota and then in Alaska, Vanballenberghe gave freely of his time and expertise in the proof reading of the rough manuscript. To both Vic Vanballenberghe and Bob Stephenson I offer my most sincere thanks.

My close friend Dr. R. Dale Guthrie, Professor of Zoology at the University of Alaska, Fairbanks, provided a colorfully understandable account of the paleontology of the gray wolf, without which my book would have lacked the depth which I hope it will offer those who read it.

Pete Haggland brought to the book a lifetime spent observing wolves in Alaska. Through the years Pete has been indispensable to researchers who have sought the truth about the gray wolf.

My special thanks must also go to Jim Smith, recently of Homer, Alaska, who spent many years trapping wolves in the territory claimed by the St. George Creek pack; to Ron Long, well-known professional trapper in Alaska's interior, and to Henry Nashookpuk of Pt. Hope, Alaska, Eskimo hunter extraordinaire and close friend.

There were many others such as Gaylen Searles of Anaktuvuk Pass, Alaska; Jim Dixon, and Jay Hammond, a long-time friend and governor of the 49th state.

Two very capable women also contributed immeasurably to the production of *The Red Snow*. My wife Ida once again gave me personal encouragement while supplying her time and ability in the final typing of the manuscript as well as an endless supply of coffee. Sally Arteseros, Senior Editor with Doubleday provided advice and a brand of professionalism that all writers should be privileged to encounter at least once during their lifetimes. She also provided that intangible ingredient without which no book could be produced. It is called simple patience.

Finally, I am indebted to Margaret Murie of Moose, Wyoming, for her willingness to write the foreword for *The Red Snow*. Her name and qualifications need no introduction to those of us who are acquainted with her background. Both Margaret and her late husband Olaus spent much of their lives in the Arctic. Like me they came to love it along with the vast natural legacy it continues to provide for all Americans.

James Greiner/Fairbanks, Alaska 1980

FOREWORD

I remember my first wolf. He was silver-gray; he was trotting unconcernedly through the short willows along the banks of Alaska's Porcupine River. From our motorboat out in midstream we watched and admired. Later in the season, coming back downriver, we camped on a gravel bar (the mosquito season was over) and in the dusk, from across the river atop a high bluff, came a musical howling I shall never forget.

I remember too the gray wolf crossing a still-frozen lake in the Brooks Range in early June. And the black one, hunting along the banks of the Toklat River in Mount McKinley National Park.

The overpowering impression and belief from all these were, and are, that *they belong there*.

We know as fact, of course, that the lives of the first men were continuously and necessarily intertwined with those of the animals that shared their habitat. It is natural, then, that through the ages there has grown a great mass of legend, of saga, of fairy tales, about animals and man. Perhaps no animal plays a larger part in this folk drama than does the wolf.

And, perhaps because somehow the wolf learned how to survive, he became a folk villain, in most stories, rather than a folk hero.

So it is refreshing, and in my belief important, to have between the covers of a book a life history of wolves which portrays them not as heroes, not as villains, not as half-manlike creatures, but simply as they are: wild animals, admirable, efficient, beautiful, that have learned the intricate and demanding laws of survival. As the author says:

". . . more than any other animal in the Arctic, wolves are a product of their rearing."

That rearing we learn about in this book. I am delighted that here the wolves are never "personalized." Yet their daily doings become so compelling that we follow them gladly.

An old man and a pack of wolves. Can a book be written with such a cast of characters? What is the plot? Can a tale be told, a moral pointed?

Yes, and much more. Along with the flow of four seasons in a comparatively small region of Alaska's vastness, we learn a great deal of the life history of all the other characters in the story: moose, caribou, bear, wolverine, fox, lynx, porcupine, rabbit, and many others, all a part of the story of the wolves, and the man.

James Greiner leaves it to us, to you and to me, to puzzle out the impact of the story. For my part, I am glad that, despite all of man's efforts, in the end there is a beginning, so that, as the author says: ". . . the gray wolf is not only alive but well in the vast wilderness that is Alaska."

Margaret E. Murie
Moose, Wyoming

For my mother

THE RED SNOW

✣ INTRODUCTION

The story of the St. George Creek wolves is factually true. Only the existence of the pack itself is fictional, while the places in which its members spend one calendar year of their brief lives are real places just as the events which transpire are true events.

During the course of the three years required to write their story, I was often asked, "Whose side are you on—the wolves' or the old man who seeks them?" I will let the reader decide for himself.

The Red Snow is not intended to create new controversies or to add fuel to the old one that has rapidly made the gray wolf a cause célèbre not only for millions of outdoor enthusiasts but for urbanites whose only glimpse of a wolf has come as a result of a visit to a museum or zoo. It is, however, an account which, for the first time, presents the wolf as he truly is, a magnificently fascinating part of our rapidly disappearing wild legacy.

Wolves are not human, despite the inferences of modern fiction, nor are they any more noble than the other big predators that still roam the land. They are, however, possessors of a complex, instinct-directed ability to organize their complex lives within the rather strict confines of a highly functional social system. Few other animals do this, with the exception of the Australian dingo and the African Cape hunting dog.

It was my intense desire to describe the life-style of the gray wolf in a form that would share the drama and excitement which are part of that life-style along with the hardships, ordinary bad luck, and reliance upon the land that wolves fall heir to. In my search for research material and during many years spent reading about wolves for pleasure, I found that most available writings are scientifically done and consist of rather unpalatable descriptions of the habits of the animal, which, in fact, could not survive were it not for his colorful, exciting, and often violent life-style.

The events that are catalogued continue to take place even as the reader experiences them, and they will do so for many years to come, for the gray wolf is not only alive but well, in the vast wilderness that is Alaska.

Among those men who share this wilderness with the wolf are individuals such as Jake Tatum who with the passage of time have found themselves members of a unique but dying breed. Their interest in the big predators stems from a lifetime of utilization rather than from our modern concern for the wolf's well-being. As such, they may seem callously crude and careless in their attitudes toward the animal that has become a symbol of latter-day exploitation by contemporary Americans. It is, however, easy for us to forget that most of our parents either subscribed to the worthless expenditure of bounty money or simply ignored the animal that was used to earn it.

The Red Snow is, then, the story of wolves and men, for the two have become inseparable. The events that occur are based upon personal observation and the aforementioned wealth of scientifically organized fact that stems from the observations of many others. The old man exists as a composite of men I have known and associated with during my own lifetime. Fortunately, or unfortunately, Jake Tatum's own life-style was doomed long ago under the influence of overwhelming pressures developed and then refined during our present generation.

It is my sincere hope that the reader will enjoy the story of this wolf pack that exemplifies uncounted hundreds of others. It is a graphically explicit account of how they live amid the controversies that their many constituents have unknowingly created.

James Greiner
Fairbanks, Alaska

❧ CHAPTER 1

A solitary raven spiraled slowly against the window of sky framed by the ravine's upper walls, its wings luffing softly in the cold afternoon stillness. Missing flight feathers formed clearly visible slots as the bird hung motionless on the waning updrafts, then disappeared as it swung away from the ledge rocks on folded wings only to return once more. Nothing moved in the gloom below, yet it was as if the black carrion eater were reluctant to leave its vantage point above the drainage.

Blue slabs of rotting glacier ice still clung to the winter-wet rocks above the bed of St. George Creek, and the flow of black water was shriveling visibly with the quickly dropping evening temperature. During midday the canyon had boomed with the sound of tumbling water, its volume fed by a feeble early May sun from the vast snowfields above. Now only the metallic trickling remained, and even this would be frozen to silence with the coming of the spring twilight, leaving thin lacelike shells of rime ice capping the slate-colored rocks.

The creek, like hundreds of others, flowed insignificantly from its origins in the ponderous north wall of the rugged Alaska Mountain Range. Totally dependent upon annual snowfall, it was fattened by glacial melt and the liquification of countless tons of decaying snow during the brief Arctic spring. By midsummer it would not be a creek at all, only a dry bed of bleached pebbles and rusted rock brought to intermittent life by infrequent rainsqualls as they pelted the barren slopes above.

Farther down the drainage, and out of sight around its final bend above the valley floor, a broad shale field received the sporadic contributions of St. George Creek, splitting and further subdividing them among the ice-scarred dwarf willows along its lower edge. Then lower still, and after being absorbed by the loose rock, the creek emerged from its brief underground ramblings saturated with silt and buckskin brown in color. Finally, after reforming in a common bed, it flowed haltingly onto the flats toward its confluence with the bigger Wood River.

The Wood, one of several large streams which bisected the lowlands, flowed in a northwesterly direction to eventually merge with the broad and sluggish Tanana as it meandered toward its own union with the mighty Yukon. Then still later, and more than eight hundred miles from its birthplace in the rocks of the Alaska Range, St. George Creek became an unnoticeable part of the Bering Sea.

This day in May had been little different from those which preceded it. Beneath a sour-bisquit-dough sky, only the damp wind from the flats had served as an almost unnoticed reminder that sixty-below-zero temperatures were once more a thing of the recent past. Spring had been slow in coming, even by Alaskan standards, and the weak, infrequent sun had served only to send scurrying spots of brilliance across the mountain slopes, bringing the siksiks, or • parka squirrels, from their burrows for brief periods during midday. Patches of granular snow still lingered beneath shadowed ledges in the bottom of gullies and beneath the stands of black spruce at the foot of the slopes.

To both the eye and ear, the ravine which carried St.

George Creek seemed devoid of all life, as though stunned by the returning cold of late afternoon. Only the occasional glassy tinkle of frost-dislodged shale broke the silence which hung like a mantle over the drainage, a silence made even more complete by thin tendrils of fog which condensed beneath the last vestige of warm air as it slid over the cold of the creekbed itself. Even the orange and red smears of lichen that added meager color to a world of rock had faded to drabness, bespectacled by water droplets which glazed to hardness even as they formed.

The wolf was a drifting blot of gray as she ascended the ravine, her winter-long claws rasping faintly as she slipped on the ice-sheathed rocks. Not trotting as wolves usually do, she seemed to move in a leisurely manner, but her panting and sagging belly betrayed the illusion. Pregnant with what would likely be her last litter of pups, she stopped frequently to sniff the invisible trail she followed among the rocks and broken tapestries of blue ice. Then, after slipping badly, she paused to lick her pendulous udders, which were tender with the traveling she had done during the long afternoon.

The bitch was small by the standards of her kind. Even given the fluids and life that bloated her, along with the bellyful of rotting caribou flesh she had consumed, her weight was less than sixty-five pounds. Had it not been for her advanced pregnancy, she would have preferred to feed at night, but hunger dictated otherwise.

There were six adult wolves in the St. George Creek pack, including the little gray bitch. A huge black male, her conjugal mate since her first period of annual heat, was as much an exception to standard size as was the small female. During times of seasonal prime, he weighed almost 130 pounds and stood three feet high at his roached shoulder. There was little doubt that his physical size and age were factors which established him as leader of the pack, yet his position of dominance was not absolute. Though he bore undisputed authority over most of the others, his mate, the small gray bitch, was also an influential member of the St. George Creek pack. Though she respected and followed him, her reaction to his dominance within the group was less rigid, and was probably a normal result of both her sex and the fact that he was her full brother.

Two buff-tan males, both two-year-old sons of the black leader and the gray bitch, formed the hunting nucleus of the pack in company with their sire. With the passage of their second winter of life and recent sexual maturity, they had attained true adulthood.

The remaining members of the St. George Creek pack were adult females. Each bore the white coloration of their common father, and were the only members of the pack that did not claim the bloodlines of the black leader.

Whelped during a heavy rainstorm which flooded the den occupied by their mother before she had licked them dry, they were the only survivors in a litter of seven pups. Then, during their second winter, both of their parents fell victim to an experienced trapper, and the pair had left their home range on the bleak MacCombe Plateau more than eighty straight-line miles to the east of St. George Creek. They had traveled alone during the balance of a severe winter, and during the following spring joined with the small group led by the black.

The merger was a rarity, for seldom do wolves join the packs of other leaders, or, more properly, are they allowed to join by the strange pack. Sheer coincidence may have been the catalyst for acceptance, as one of the white bitches was in estrus when the wolves met, while the other had just finished with her own heat period.

The small size of the black's pack may also have been responsible for his giving reluctant permission to the white wolves to first follow at a respectable distance and then finally be accepted as regular members of the St. George Creek pack. Had either or both these circumstances been absent, it is more than likely that the big wolf and his adult sons would have routed the strangers or even killed them.

Both were, as a result of the absence of parents during their second year, more inexperienced where hunting was concerned than they would have been after a more normal adolescence. As resident members of the pack, they occupied the lower end of the social order headed by the huge black but more rigidly enforced by his mate, the gray bitch.

Two days earlier the black wolf had led the others away from the remnants of the caribou carcass in search of better meat, and upon his return he would continue to aid his two adult sons in the care of his pregnant mate. Since the pack's departure, the gray bitch had made several of the five-mile journeys to the carcass, seemingly content with the nearness of her solitary meals.

Several foxes, a dozen or more of the ubiquitous ravens, and a wolverine competed with her for what was left of the more than two hundred pounds of meat that the caribou had once represented. The foxes required and ate little, while the ravens consumed surprising quantities of the softening flesh, and the bearlike wolverine seemed obsessed only with a stolid ambition to carry away every last scrap, eating only occasionally while present at the kill.

The wolverine had left scuffling trails which led to all points of the compass away from the kill, and while dragging each chunk of meat and hide, he had paused only long enough to hastily chew away those parts of his booty that became tangled in the stunted willows. His efforts that afternoon resulted in the disappearance of the entire antlered head as he resolutely dragged the twenty-pound burden to a point more than half a mile from the carcass. Each cache of meat he established was doused with his sour musky urine, then buried beneath patchy loose snow and thawing earth, to be exhumed at some later date. That the wolverine would forget the location of virtually all these morsels was of little concern to him, and his shortsightedness was surpassed only by his exceedingly foul disposition.

During the two days just past, the forty-pound animal had visited the carcass while the gray bitch dozed nearby, and she had tolerated his presence. The short-legged, chocolate-brown animal moved constantly as he fed, the yoke-shaped mantle of long yellowish guard hairs over his hips and flanks rippling as he worked at the carcass. Reluctant to feed while the pack was in attendance, he watched the sleeping bitch with small hazel-colored eyes while grunting shallowly with the effort required to work chunks of frost-marbled flesh from the rotting carcass. The foxes possessed far less courage than did the wolverine and a mere fraction of his ambition. They vacated the kill when the gray bitch approached and returned only after she departed.

Eleven years of life had been an eternity for the small gray bitch, a span punctuated regularly by events which had taught habit patterns rooted in momentary incidents of panic sometimes coupled with physical pain. As she continued her slow climb of the darkening creekbed, her slight limp became obvious and she flinched involuntarily at some imagined threat.

Once clear of the drainage's steepest part, and following a vague sheep trail which snaked among the dead, snow-matted grass and dwarf willows, she began to trot steadily. Then, higher on the clearing, tendrils of vapor obscured her as she covered the final quarter mile to the domelike promontory which housed the den. Located well away from the rocky bed of St. George Creek in a hanging treeless meadow, its mouth was made visible only as she paused to enter it.

Dug by foxes during some long-past time, the den was set twelve feet deep beneath the meadow's skin of powdery, acid soil. Slanting downward for almost eight feet through glacial debris, it turned at right angles to the main passageway before ending abruptly in a cul-de-sac only slightly larger than the small wolf. The den had no other entrances or exits. The soil surrounding the den chamber itself consisted of powdered rock fines, and because of its elevation and origin, was free of permafrost. As such, it was dry, a fact which long ago made the site acceptable to those who used it.

The floor of the den was littered with use-worn pebbles and small sticks, but was devoid of bones and other debris. It was a place of total darkness, to be used by scent and feel alone. The gray bitch knew it well, for she had whelped here during all but two of the nine springs that had passed since her first heat period.

Above ground, the den's mouth was hidden among the nodding tufts of wiry sedges and porous slab rock that covered the entire dome, and was nearly invisible. Even the shelf of loose soil kicked out by the early generations of red and cross foxes that created the excavation in the beginning had begrudgingly accepted the infinitely slow growth of moss, lichens, and saw grass, so that only the deep-cut and narrow trail which vanished into the mouth of the den set the place apart from the rest of the hillside. On this day in mid-May it was the only one of four others above the creek that was occupied for the purpose of birth, for the St. George Creek pack boasted only one pregnancy this year.

Though she had never brought food here, the interior of the den reeked with the scent of the caribou carcass that saturated her coat, for it was beginning to decompose in the scant warmth of the lengthening days. Due to her advanced pregnancy, the gray bitch had rested frequently while feeding among the slatted rib bones and other debris which protruded through the snow. At other times she moved away, sometimes several hundred feet distant, to lay up in a more preferable position, one usually open to the sun's warmth and at an elevation higher than the kill.

With use, the site of the kill had become hard-packed, the snow stained brown with blood and yellowed by the scattered oily contents of the caribou's paunch. If seen from above, the place would have resembled a huge wagon wheel, the carcass itself forming the hub, and trails made by the gray bitch and other visitors to the kill, the spokes, which radiated outward in numerous directions.

The St. George Creek pack had merely been the final mechanism which brought death to the caribou, and its carcass had represented a gratuity not to be passed by. The barren, spindle-antlered cow had, in fact, already been dead on its feet of simple old age coupled with the long-term inroads of stomach parasites as she stumbled out onto the remnant snow pan that fanned away from the tiny creek. Open-mouthed and panting, she sought escape from the heat of the spring sun, heat made oppressive by her thick, dull, and as yet unshed winter coat of hollow hair. Each spring during her long lifetime had held similar periods of suffering the sudden need to adapt physiologically to a brief world of heat after seven months of absolute cold. Lying on the slushy snow seemed to reduce the added torture perpetrated by the already present clouds of tiny gnats, and it is likely that she would not have fled even had she been able to regain her feet fast enough to avoid the wolves that smothered her.

For the pack, the cow had represented an easily attained supply of fresh meat, and the short five-mile distance that separated it from the den made it more than accessible to the gray bitch. Had the winter just past been more severe, the entire pack would easily have consumed the carcass during the first day of the kill, but travel was easy and game becoming plentiful. The black had fed lightly, as did the others, after which they struck out across the pans of granular snow and thaw-drenched reaches of open tundra to hunt elsewhere. The gray bitch had not accompanied the pack.

Because of her advanced pregnancy, the old female continued to placate her insatiable hunger here. For her the carcass was a bounty in a land that offered few, while for the solitary wolverine it was merely a luxury to be gloated over and hoarded in well-fed greed, then ultimately wasted through simple forgetfulness.

Were the small gray bitch of fewer years and shorter experience, it is likely that she would, by now, be well on her way to a slow, almost imperceptible death by starvation. Her gimped hind leg, her small size, and badly worn teeth, coupled with the pregnancy, which, because of her age, should not have occurred, would have tipped the delicate scales long before. Only her inclusion in the black male's young constituency had made this, her eleventh summer, possible.

Yawning in the darkness of the den, she nipped at her tufted flanks in an idle effort to still the kicking pups, then shifted her position among the smooth, hair-matted irregularities of the den floor. Though she had visited the caribou carcass daily, her meals there had become hurried, almost urgent, and as a result she had spent increasing periods of time in the den. Each day during the past week, the trip back had become more burdensome, and today her labored panting persisted long after she had regained her wind.

Above and beyond her sight, the den opening had winked out, and her ears flicked as a small bridge of ice collapsed somewhere in the darkness of rocks above the meadow. Then, after turning several times and finding no comfort in the doing, she stood bent-legged in the total darkness before scratching at the unyielding floor of the den.

CHAPTER 2

I f one were to stand upon the gentle slope two miles below the den, the point at which St. George Creek breaks free of the mountains, and look to the northwest, he would see a broad, seemingly flat valley. Sixty miles beyond that point, the softly veiled outlines of the Tanana Hills gently stop the eye, then abruptly lose their shape to the viewer's left. Beyond, there is only unbroken distance as the valley of the Tanana River widens to be bisected by the far-off and unseen Yukon. Only one landmark remains, and even this is finally absorbed by the hazy miles. It is the continuation of the same mountain chain which towers steeply behind the observer, the Alaska Range, an upthrusting wall of chimneyed rock spires which belt the girth of the forty-ninth state as they cross a span of more than 750 miles before ending in the far-flung Aleutian Chain.

Alaska is a vast land, and despite controversies stemming from the publicizing of recent oil development and other signs of human progress, it is still inhospitable and much of it virtually inaccessible. The 7,500 square miles which comprise the flats of the interior valley are but a minuscule portion of the whole, and though none is apparent, an order which reflects the flats' origins exists here.

Today, the flats consist of silty rivers, whiskey-colored

creeks, impenetrable bogs tufted with clumps of upstanding
saw-grass-coifed soil and sedge-matted stagnant ponds. The
flats are a true wilderness, carpeted irregularly with cold-
dwarfed black spruce, laced with alder and willow jungles,
and picketed with bleached tree skeletons. Dead and fallen
timber form a mat where wind, heavy snow, shifting river-
beds, and wildfires have torn shallow root systems from
the powdery, silt-based soil. It is the range of the gray wolf
bitch and hundreds more like her, yet a mere fourteen thousand years ago it was a dry, treeless grassland.

The Alaska Range is a young chain of mountains, one
which is still in the process of thrusting upward into the
pale Arctic sky at a rate which has slackened little since formation began many millions of years ago.

In the beginning, earth existed as a spinning gaseous
sphere which liquified as it slowly cooled. As its temperature
dropped, a thin skinlike crust of basalt began to form. This
scum then hardened slowly, to become a floating mass of
broad, islandlike tectonic plates. Later, because of the
earth's rotational movement, the wanderings of these plates
became predictable, and their swirling pathway toward the
northeast left telltale evidence of their passage in the form
of mountains which formed in their wake. The earth still has
a molten core which supports a cooling layer, or mantle, of
such plates. The passage of the millenia has thickened them,
but they are still moving, as evidenced by the hundreds of
earthquakes which reverberate through the remote Arctic
each year, and in the mountains which continue to grow.

In the beginning, violent collisions along the edges of the
floating plates caused them to buckle vertically, and it was
this early phenomenon which resulted in the birth of the
mountains. Unimaginable pressures from both within and
beneath caused thousands of square miles of the place that
would later be called Alaska to rupture vertically along a
southwesterly line. The shape of the land that we know and

recognize easily today did not exist then, and only the embryonic mountain ranges rose from the level that would later be defined by the surface of oceans. Finally, with continued cooling, the floating basalt scum became a shell, but was still tortured by earthquakes and volcanoes.

Alaska was already a contiguous mass long before it reached the place on the globe that it now occupies. It was, however, farther south, and layers of rock in the Alaska Mountains offer evidence that a subtropical climate once existed. Coral reefs left telltale contributions to the geological record, and hint that during the passage of a few more seconds in the evolutionary clock, primitive palm trees and exotic ferns once thrived here. It was during this period that the creatures we call prehistoric began to walk the earth.

Paleontological time is a concept that relies upon numbers so large that they stagger the imagination. A million years is far beyond our ability to comprehend and appreciate, as is a mere thousand, yet one must grapple with such quantities when attempting to understand the time span over which wolves have lived upon the earth. If slightly fewer than forty million pennies were stacked, one upon the other, they would form a column approximately forty miles high. Then, if each penny in such a stack were arbitrarily designated as a calendar year, we would still find the relationship virtually impossible to grasp, yet for more than forty million years the wolf has been evolving on this continent.

Forty million years ago diminutive creatures that paleontologists call the Miacidae had already been developing for ten millenia. One form bore carnassial or "flesh" teeth, and in this single characteristic, a vague early resemblance to the gray wolf. It was from this rather unlikely common parent that not only wolves but other meat eaters such as the lynx, bear, weasel, and even the domestic dog would eventually spring.

With the passage of additional eons, but still twenty million years ago, one form began to stand out among the others. He has come to be known as tomarctus, and even at that early time would have been easily recognizable as a principal forerunner of modern-day wolves. Larger than the gray wolf, his hind legs were longer and his feet more compact. One of his toes had already become rudimentary, and its vestige persists today as the dew claw, a useless appendage which clings to the upper rear surface of the forelegs of both wolves and domestic dogs. Tomarctus was the first true wolf.

Five million years later, foxes sprang from the tomarctus strain, after which the lineage of the wolves became defined so specifically that development continued uninterrupted through modern time. Thus, fifteen million years ago, the early wolf was here, yet 14,985,000 more years were destined to pass before man would see him and then quickly learn the art of domesticating him to produce the ubiquitous household pet so well known to us all.

The Bering Land Bridge, which has periodically connected the North American Arctic with Siberia, separated for the last, or at least most recent, time about fourteen thousand years ago. Rising water produced by melting glaciers which formed after the Alaskan land mass reached its present northerly position changed the shape of the entire globe, and it was at this time that the outline of Alaska emerged.

It is doubtful that man's passage across the flat plain called the land bridge was a spontaneous event, and probable that he used it for many years prior to its last separation fourteen thousand years ago. If such indeed is the case, however, no real evidence exists to support the theory. It is known that the short, tan-skinned creature that walked upright and possessed the ability to sew animal skins to produce clothing to protect him from a harsh climate that was little different than that which exists today in the Arctic was here when his route back to the land he had left was cut off.

As the land mass destined to become Alaska shifted northward, it assumed a colder annual climate. This occurred long before man ever saw it. The lush vegetation of the earlier, warmer millenia had already been replaced by hardier species such as hemlock and other needle-bearing trees. And then even this changed. Where verdant forests had stood, the vast valley floors became seas of wind-whipped grass, a condition that prevailed when the sea separated the Asian and North American continents for the last time. It was at this point that lesser terrain features such as the Tanana Hills of the interior took form as deposits of dust and rock fines, which settled when the strong prevailing winds dissipated.

One hundred and forty centuries ago seems to be a handy place to begin the story of the gray wolf, providing one does not forget the fact that he was here for more than fourteen million years before that in a form virtually identical to the one in which he appears today. The wolf has always been a predator, and before the appearance of grasslands in Alaska he had successfully competed with other hunters such as the jackel-like dole, the short-faced bear, the lion, and even the awesome saber-toothed tiger.

Since his role as a hunter remained virtually unchanged through the ages, the wolf became a highly flexible survivor. With the coming of the grasslands, other species which relied specifically upon forest prey began to disappear, seemingly unable to adapt to hunting the grazing animals which replaced the forest dwellers. That the wolf was successful in this venture is obvious, for today, in spite of man's intrusion and sometimes misplaced concern, he exists in numbers which may very well surpass those of fourteen thousand years ago.

He quickly learned how to hunt hairy mammoth calves, primitive bison, camels, sheep, wild ponies and donkeys, and other grass-eating ungulate prey species. Though there were others that competed with him for survival on the treeless land, none was more impressive than the gray wolf's close relative, the dire wolf. Though the latter possessed a massive lower jaw, he competed with the gray wolf only after the kill had been made, a kill which he seldom helped consummate, for the dire wolf was a carrion eater by choice.

The land continued to change. Vast plains began to disappear and with continuation of the cycle came the inexorable disappearance of those animals that depended upon grass for survival. Then as the plentitude of grazing prey species shriveled, the dire wolf came upon hard times, and he too vanished from the scene. The gray wolf remained, however, and today is the undisputed king among the large Arctic predators, as much at home on the barren treeless tundra as he is among the spruces and down timber of the interior.

Where they had flourished, the grassy plains left a thin layer of humus, and with the glaciers melting once more in a climate that had warmed, the water table once more lifted. Though these conditions were slow in maturing, they eventually provided a place where scrubby dwarf birch and willow could take root and colonize the north. The cycle was repeating itself, and in time, needle-bearing trees once more carpeted the big land. It was a trend which resulted in the boggy, impenetrable landscape which is typical of Alaska's interior reaches today.

Only the mountains have sustained their original mode of formation, one which continues at the present time. During the last eight thousand years, the peaks of the Alaska Range have grown many hundreds of feet. As the range continues to thrust itself upward, pulling the valley with it, it has also disgorged itself onto the flatlands at its base. Hence, the Tanana Flats are not flat at all, but tilt gently toward the mountains. Because of this gradient, rivers which course from the drainages that perforate the lower slopes of the range exist as straight channels rather than as meandering stream beds. Once clear of the containing mountains, melted water gains velocity rapidly in these channels, gouging them deeply into the land. The banks of such streams are high and shelf-like, and during the short spring, with the thawing snow, the water which chokes them rumbles with rolling rocks and heavy gravel, a broth of evolutionary dust.

Compared with the gray wolf, man is a very recent newcomer to the Arctic, yet even he has been here for an impressive period of time. Archaeologists have discovered his fire pits, smears of carbon buried beneath countless tons of overburden. They have also dug up his bones and some of his possessions. More recently, they have discovered his ornately carved spearpoints. Yet such materials provide only a scant record of his being, a record which ends abruptly about eleven thousand years ago. Was man in the Arctic before that time? Archaeologists believe that he was.

Today, the Bering Land Bridge that ancient man must have crossed is buried beneath the shallow, cold waters of the northern Pacific Ocean. The tiny Diomedes, King, St. Lawrence, and St. Mathews islands are among the last vestiges of the dry ground which once connected two continents with a flat, savannahlike plain. It was, as it still is, a bleak place, whipped by constant gale-velocity winds generated over the ice-locked Arctic Ocean. Carpeted with grass and sedges, it was cloaked almost year-round by dense fog and pelted with icy rain squalls in a manner identical to that which exists along the Aleutian Chain today.

It is known that man was here and had already established himself eleven thousand years ago, and it seems probable that he was here before that time. It is also logical to assume that, from his westerly landfall, he moved inland and that he met the gray wolf. Why man came here and how he survived are questions which have long fascinated modern generations. One fact stands clear—the ancients were hunters of supreme ability. They possessed a refined technology which provided functional weapons and crudely tailored garments made from the skins of animals they killed. Most astounding is the fact that they accomplished all of this in a land where, in its northern reaches, bitter winters lasted virtually all year, as they still do. Like the gray wolf, early man in Alaska was an adaptive competitor, and because of this, he too has survived to the present time.

As the forebears of the modern Alaskan native peoples moved eastward into the interior, they discovered a land in transition. Though not true nomads, they moved with opportunistic purpose on a seasonal basis. Such movement occurred within shifting territories, and was triggered by changing game populations. Also like the wolf, early man quickly learned that to follow was to survive.

The Danish navigator Vitus Bering saw Alaska in the year 1728 from the heaving deck of his ship *St. Gabriel*. It was perhaps ironic that he first sighted it while navigating the waters which by then obscured the land bridge. He saw an island which was later called St. Lawrence, but did not see the mainland. Later, in 1741, he sailed once more to the southeast from Siberia, and this time made landfall in southern Alaska. The contact period had begun.

A brief 150 years after Bering's discovery, the natives of Alaska changed their traditional life-style under the persistent influence of white missionaries. They became village people, thus accepting the inevitable change from seminomadic hunters living in scattered winter settlements to permanent year-round habitation. Modern Alaska is indeed a very young land.

Because of familiarity, the Alaskan native sees the gray wolf through different eyes than does his white counterpart. As a result, even among the impressionable Eskimos and Indians of the big land, the wolf has never become the creature of legend that Caucasians have demanded. The native learned during the passage of thousands of years to share the land with the wolf, and to compete but never dominate. It is, perhaps, the final irony that the wolf has lived here for at least fourteen million years, the native for more than fourteen thousand, and white man for a mere seventy-five, yet it is the latter who seems bent upon the task of domination.

Still, the legend that surrounds the gray wolf prospers. It is a legend that came north with the early sourdoughs and gold seekers just after the turn of this century, a legend that continues to grow in direct proportion to the shrinking range of the animal which catalyzes it.

Early white explorers and exploiters feared the land itself. During their first Arctic winter, few escaped the lonely depression of forced exile in a hostile land, and it followed that they would fear the one animal that tradition had erroneously taught them was hostile and even aggressive to strangers.

The Arctic, with its limitless reaches, brittle cold, endless winter nights illuminated only by the pastel tapestry of the aurora, and the forced privation shared by men in a strange land where survival was the only game around, was a strong catalyst for the perpetuation of a legend. It is easy to imagine the red glitter of wolves' eyes reflecting the light cast by campfires, and natural to envision the fear that chance encounters with the wolf engendered as these early travelers clung to the bracing and lines of their dogsleds pulled by a team gone wild as it encountered a wolf along the trail.

The small gray bitch that slept fitfully beneath the surface of the hanging meadow above St. George Creek had already spent more than a decade surviving on the land where she was born. Eleven years among gray wolves is a life-span seldom attained, yet was but a fleeting second in the history of that land. How she got here, or even the fact that she had already lived longer than most others of her kind, was, of course, unrecognized and therefore unimportant to her. That she was here was not even a conscious realization. Last year had already faded from her recollection, and only the growing, cramplike spasms in her gut were of any real significance at all.

CHAPTER 3

Spring in the Alaskan interior barely qualifies as a well-defined season of the year. Rather, it consists of an almost unnoticed transitional period between winter's bitter darkness and a full-blown but breathtakingly brief summer which flickers and dies after three short months of twenty-four-hour daylight. Its coming is heralded by nothing more than a few weeks of warming temperatures, wind which no longer carries the breath-sucking chill of late winter, and, finally, by bitter rainsqualls that sweep across the rotting snow. True summer often arrives, quite literally, overnight.

Rivers, creeks, and freshets that begrudgingly began to flow only in the more temperate daylight suddenly cascade almost uninterrupted throughout the shortening nighttime hours, and new leaves burst through catkins and resin-coated buds on the willows that produced them even before the snow has fully melted at their bases. Such a change occurred during the night the black male and the rest of the pack returned to the St. George Creek den meadow.

The nervous spasms which gripped the gray bitch and caused her to dig instinctively at the floor of the den chamber had subsided, and she had slept lightly for several hours. Then, though awakened by the snuffling of her mate at the den entrance above, she did not climb the passageway to the surface as she would have on most other occasions. Whining thinly as the sniffing of the big leader stopped, she sighed raggedly before turning several times and curling up once more, her long snout tucked under her plumed tail.

Though the small mountain valley which concealed the den was still locked in shadow, the upper reaches of the range itself glowed in the pale orange light of early morning. The air had become noticeably warmer during the twilight hours, and a tepid breeze washed the slope above St. George Creek. It carried the smells of the far-off flats, and, as if to confirm the change that had occurred, the creek tunked hollowly with rushing water long before the night frost darkened and melted on the rocks that jutted above its bed.

The gray bitch joined the group above ground just as the first slanting rays of warmth glittered blindingly from the crests of the high shale ridges. She paused only long enough to touch the black male's nose as he trotted to meet her before going to the icy creek, where she lapped greedily.

The big wolf had returned from his most recent travels bearing a sparsely fleshed leg bone from the caribou remnants below the den. He had paused there to feed hastily after an unsuccessful night of hunting, as had those that accompanied him, and his gift to the female was the result of an instinctive habit which he indulged in on a regular basis, as did his buff sons.

At her approach, the black dropped the leg bone in front of the gray bitch, but she paid little attention to the gesture or to the decomposed bluish flesh that clung to the femur. The old bitch was not hungry for the first time in several weeks, but the fact made no conscious impression upon her as she retraced her steps to the mouth of the den. Reaching it, and after ignoring the playful advances of the larger of her buff-colored sons, she flopped on her side to regain her breath and allow the warmth of the rising sun to penetrate her winter-dense coat.

The gray bitch was more at home beneath the St. George Creek meadow than in any other part of her vast range, an area which exceeded six hundred square miles. She had successfully raised twenty-five pups here and, without plan, accepted the drainage as the epicenter of her territory, as did the rest of the pack. The group had grown and shrunk in size over the long years, at one time boasting fourteen adult members during the black male's yearling winter.

The warm breeze continued to flood the dome as the sun climbed above the peaks behind the old female. The scents from the Tanana Flats almost two thousand feet below the den caused her nostrils to dilate constantly even as she dozed, and her ears twitched in their unceasing, involuntary efforts to forestall the first of thousands of tiny gnats that had come to life in the rapidly warming air. The black leader slept soundly ten feet below her position, his legs moving spasmodically as they still responded to the trotting stimulus that had worked without letup as he had covered more than a hundred miles since departing the den. The remaining four wolves were scattered within a radius of several dozen yards.

Raising her head slightly, the gray bitch took in the scene with her yellow-brown eyes. Though her mate was two seasons younger, he was her full brother, a fact which had never and would never intrude upon her consciousness. It was even possible that the general good health of the progenies she had already produced during her long lifetime was directly attributable to this inbreeding, for it is an irrefutable fact that such genetic combinations either succeed brilliantly or fail in abject misery. Like other brood females, the gray bitch had lost her share of pups over the years, but never as a result of congenital malformation. Unlike those of a few others, none of her offspring had been scarred before parturition by the rare, grotesque underslung jaws, cleft palates, and other abnormalities resulting from close interfamily cohabitation in other species. The process is one upon which the gray wolf thrives.

The complex and many-faceted system which governs such processes in the wild quickly and effectively weeds out mutants and other deviations from the norm, and though rare among wolves, puppies bearing such genetic backgrounds are quickly eliminated by death either during birth or shortly thereafter. The system limits itself, however, and the chances of success drop off dramatically in successive generations. Regardless of, and perhaps because of, this difficult-to-define behavioral norm, one truth stands clear— few in-betweens exist in the world of the gray wolf, and one of the most basic necessities for survival beyond the complex society of the pack is functional physical well-being.

Yet, in spite of the necessity of a sound body with which to start life, wolves are capable of functioning under physical adversity. Paws crushed and broken by traps heal, and limitations from teeth shattered on the steel of such traps during long hours of chewing required to gain release are somehow overcome. Even blindness, unless it is total, is an assumed imperfection to which wolves can somehow adapt. Such animals must rely upon the support of a healthy, well-knit pack for survival, however, and to this rule there seem to be few exceptions.

The gray bitch whine-yawned, then stretched to her full length, her tail curving upward and back across her narrow hips, after which she nipped at the bony foot of her gimped leg. It was a hot day. The sun, its rays undiluted in the rarefied mountain air, had slowly moved to a position overhead. As its heat became real, she panted with the excessive warmth that was aggravated by her dense winter coat. With the passage of a few more weeks, she would begin to shed the woolly, cream-colored underhair that insulated her body during winter, and her flanks would be festooned with shaggy streamers of wool, making her look ragged and of poor health. For her, however, the completion of the molt would be slower than for the rest of the pack, once more due to her pregnancy and the hormone changes induced by the birth of her new litter.

The black male stirred suddenly, snapping at the gnats which clustered along his closed eyelids, inflaming them. He too felt the oppressive heat of midday, and rising, trotted resolutely downslope after being joined by both of his sons. The threesome continued across the short distance that separated the dome from a small gully which led to the tumbling creek. Before disappearing from the gray bitch's sight, one of the young wolves paused to roll vigorously in the ground willow and dry moss. It was a lazy day, one of transition, and the pack seemed to sense the final breaking of the awesome Arctic winter.

Wolves, like their domestic counterparts, seldom sleep deeply, and the gray bitch passed the long afternoon dozing and waking over brief periods. She was content to rest, idly watching the circling ravens and a Harlan's hawk whose screams awakened her on two occasions as the large, dark-colored raptor circled briefly on the updrafts over the den meadow. Except for the sound of the tumbling creek, little else intruded upon her senses. It was as though the mountains themselves were content to allow the warming rays of the late-May sun to strip the slush snow from their lowest slopes, and only the occasional showers of falling shale loosened by the thaw broke the silence among the steep ravines that stretched upward above the dozing wolf. The gray bitch caught movement below her vantage point, but it was merely one of the white resident females sitting upright to scratch vigorously. The white wolf was the only other animal in evidence on the slope.

With the slow passage of the afternoon hours, shadows cast by the surrounding peaks shifted visibly, and twilight had begun to deepen as the black male and his sons returned to the den site. On his arrival, the big leader touched the gray bitch's nose with his own, then took her muzzle into his mouth. It was a gentle act of greeting, and she rolled onto her side, acting out the age-old ritual which subtly reaffirmed subservience to her longtime mate. He was the only pack member to be accorded such homage, but in his presence it was an automatic gesture.

Above the meadow the sky had acquired a pastel salmon hue, and the air cooled quickly as the sun slipped behind the line of lesser peaks which shielded the den meadow from the flats below. The color was deepened where it touched the upper mountains, and the white-tipped guard hairs of the old bitch's coat seemed to assume the same tint. A distant flock of ptarmigan slanted along the blue-shadowed rocks which bordered the St. George Creek ravine below the den, and after watching the dozen or more white specks flicker through a still-sun-drenched portion of the valley, the gray bitch rose, stiff-legged.

During the long day she had remained disinterested in food, though she had traveled to the creek several times for water. Her belly was distended more than ever, and as she returned to the mouth of the den after her most recent visit to the creek she panted heavily. Then, while surveying the confines of the meadow, she felt the nervousness of the night before returning.

Still later, in the cooling air, the buzzing gnats swarmed, and smokelike columns of the tiny insects danced above the stunted willows along the creek. The black leader had once more left the confines of the meadow, followed by his sons and one of the white females. Only the other resident female remained, and she approached the gray bitch slowly, tentatively wagging her tail. While still a dozen feet away, she flopped over on her back to roll, seemingly content to keep some distance between herself and the older wolf. Finally, panting lightly, and disinterested in the white resident, the gray bitch turned and disappeared into the mouth of the den.

The coolness of the down-slanting passageway was an abrupt change from the warmer evening air above, and she shivered as she slid to the nest chamber. The darkness there was absolute, and her panting was the only sound as she sat on her haunches experiencing a mild form of panic, which stemmed from her growing nervousness. Several minutes passed, after which she stood and circled several times before lying down. As she did so, she popped her teeth and whined softly.

Midnight passed, and half-darkness had settled over the meadow, leaving the sky a pale lemon dome which shaded to green where it met the southwestern horizon. During the dark hours, the gray bitch made several trips to the surface, and doing so seemed to still the waves of trembling that had begun earlier. Then her stays on the surface became increasingly shorter, and though consumed by a powerful urge to quench her thirst, she did not go to the creek. She had already felt the first of the mild cramps beneath her rib cage that signaled the approaching birth of the pups she had carried for sixty-six days, three days longer than normal term. Ignoring the keening of the white female, the bitch tested the softly gusting wind, but her nose discerned only the dry, dusty freshness of moss and lichens and the ephemeral dampness of melting snow. Then her ears flicked upward and forward as they picked up the droning sound which carried from the west.

The tiny bush plane, its red and green wing lights twinkling in the dark sky to the south, was but the first of many that would pass overhead during the coming summer, yet the gray bitch flinched and looked upslope as it broke over the ridgeline. Its sound had an even flatness that was almost hypnotic, and the pregnant wolf felt the growing urge to flee that she always experienced at such times. Then she was swallowed by the mouth of the den, and only the white wolf remained exposed on the hillside as the plane passed from sight over the high peaks.

Another hour passed slowly, during which her cramps became rhythmic spasms, and the first pup was born quickly, pushed by muscle contractions so powerful that no adult wolf could have survived them. The air in the den was heavy with the brassy scent of placental fluid as the gray bitch licked the tiny, roan pup dry. She had carried this litter longer than any that had preceded it, and the lateness of the birth was probably the result of her advancing age.

Conception had occurred during the second of three couplings with her big mate as the pack had roamed the lower reaches of the Tatlanika River during early March. Unlike the term of pregnancy it had caused, however, their annual period of heat-generated courtship had been almost cursory, its brevity yet another probable signal that her long productivity was approaching its end.

Moments after the birth of the first pup, the old bitch nipped the convoluted bluish cord attached to its naked belly, a process made efficient by its very simplicity. The short, blunt-edged incisor teeth between the canines crushed the cut edges of the cord as it was severed, thus closing it, stanching the insignificant flow of blood, and thereby promoting healing.

Though she continued to lick the squirming pup, the gray bitch seemed almost disinterested in it, and two more hours passed before she once more felt the building spasms, forerunners of the second pup's birth. Then, panting rapidly in the darkness, she circled nervously, somehow avoiding the first pup with her long-clawed feet. Females of lesser experience often stepped upon their young even as the process of whelping continued, or lay upon them accidentally, yet if practice made the process of reproducing easier and more efficient, better results did not stem from conscious thought on the part of female wolves. The phenomenon of birth, though basic to all wild species, is a uniquely instinctive process, and the inherited reactions to it sharpen as each breeding and whelping season is experienced.

One of the gray bitch's buff-colored sons barked sharply outside, and the sound reached the bitch's ears as she rested during midmorning. Her labored breathing had ceased sometime after the birth of her fourth pup, and she dozed with an almost desperate need for time during which to regenerate the energy she had burned during the long night. In spite of her age and minor infirmities, the gray bitch was in good physical condition, but her sides had assumed a rib-sprung appearance with the sudden absence of the tiny one-pound forms that now nestled in the hollow made by her curled body. In the darkness she found each pup with her nose, methodically rolling them onto their backs to facilitate licking their bellies, while cleaning her own vulva, which still seeped the residual fluids of birth.

Somewhere beyond the den mouth, a raven uttered a sound akin to the dull metallic clanking of a rusted dishpan, and was answered by the short guttural calls of others as the big carrion eaters once more assumed their daily patrol of the sunlit drainage. Probably no other faunal form, except perhaps the moose of the interior, is as much an integral part of the life of gray wolves than are these ever-present Corvids, and no finer-honed coexistence occurs between wild species of the Arctic. The phenomenon is especially true in the treeless northern reaches of Alaska, where caribou form a triumvirate of survival with wolves and the big birds.

Stretching her neck until she lay flat on her side, the bitch made her udders available to the pups, udders swollen with the milk produced under the complex influence of the rapidly changing hormonal balance in her own bloodstream and the catalyzing effect of the afterbirth she had eaten.

Then, testing the slight movement of air in the den tunnel with a nose a hundred more times more powerful than man's, she sighed raggedly and once more closed her eyes.

Outside the den, a vast spectrum of life was responding to the sun, life that was rapidly transforming the flats below the St. George Creek den. Canada jays, known as whiskey jacks or camp robbers to the sourdoughs, were once more mysteriously plentiful on the flats as they swung in gliding flight between the spruces uttering their piping calls. Slate juncos swept over the punky earth between the same trees, dipping and flashing their white tail feathers. Overhead, ragged skeins of white-fronted geese, or specklebellies, gabbled like feisty dogs barking in the cirrus-domed sky as they swept westward toward the Minto Flats and north to the vast pothole-saturated valley of the Yukon River, and slowly undulating lines of whistling swans called discordantly as they too passed overhead. Nor were the mountains and their lower slopes ignored as flocks of creamy-hued buntings flared in unison over the rocks and shale washes, chattering as they raced to catch up in the overwhelming distance of the ravines.

All of these things and more had occurred across Alaska's broad interior in a few moments. The stage for the telescoping of events which would produce a mature summer season in less than two weeks had been set behind a disguise of late snowsqualls which had marched across the land a week before.

CHAPTER 4

With the birth of her pups, the daily habit patterns of the gray bitch changed abruptly. Where before the whelping she was free to leave the den at regular though decreasing intervals, she now found herself a willing slave to its confines. Though many abilities possessed by gray wolves are the product of learning, reproduction is not one of them. Like hunger and thirst, the act is based upon biological need, and is conceived and perpetuated in the simple instincts which form the basis for all such phenomena.

Following conception, these powerful drives become even stronger as the embryonic pups grow from microscopic cell clusters to the sixteen-ounce infants they are at birth. Even before whelping, the female enters into a contract with her instincts and physiology, and not until her offspring reach the age of slightly less than one year will she be released from its tenets. By then, however, she will be pregnant once more, a maternal schedule which has involved all but the first twenty-two months of the gray bitch's lifetime.

The world into which the three male pups and the single female were born was a silent place, not only because of the subterranean nature of the den, but because, like all wolf pups of their age, they were stone deaf. This fact coupled with their blindness made them almost totally unaware of the nature of their surroundings. Their rude expulsion from the bitch's body had constituted a trauma to be experienced by feel alone, for even the superb sense of smell which would come later was denied them.

All were darkly furred and reddish roan, and their blunt noses, ratty tails, and short stubby ears gave them the appearance of domestic dogs of the same age. Unlike dogs, however, the process which had, through the passing millenia, made wolves one of the most successful classes of predators had already begun, triggered by the bitch's rough tongue.

Though of little apparent consequence to their eventual adult behavior, the pups needed this attention as they needed the warmth the bitch's body provided, and after only a few hours they sought it avidly. Worming closer and seeking her breasts, they accepted a dependency that would form the very foundation of adulthood. Even the female's licking of their distended abdomens, a process which caused them to eliminate almost immediately, would be mimicked in adulthood as they flopped on their sides or backs while submitting to others. Thus, through simple training which begins at birth, the gray wolf learns a life of social dependency, a factor which defines the concept of the pack.

The gray bitch remained with her pups constantly during the three days following their birth. Not until the fourth day did she begin spending some time in the sunlight which flooded the mossy shelf above the den's mouth. During the days which slipped by almost unnoticed by the old female, the flats below the meadow continued to change dramatically, and embryonic pea-green leaves nodded in the warm breezes which washed the sea of aspen and alder along the lower reaches of St. George Creek. Only a pronounced restlessness remained as a final behavioral vestige of the change that had once more occurred in the bitch's long life, a change that had not only brought her four pups but, more important, had nearly doubled the size of the pack.

During the first week after whelping, her body weight dropped alarmingly, and it gaunted her further. Only after she began to eat the small quantities of meat brought to her by the black leader and her adult sons did her condition stabilize. Often they carried such offerings a dozen miles or more to the den, where they were accepted eagerly by the waiting bitch. The caribou carcass which provided for her minimal needs during the final weeks of her pregnancy had by now been reduced to a brownish smear which lingered in a thin plate of dirty ice because it was shaded by a sheet of parchmentlike hide and hidden from the sun's warmth. With the passage of a short time, even these paltry remains of an animal which once weighed well over two hundred pounds would disappear, the rib bones eaten or carried off by resident parka squirrels, mice, and passing porcupines, and the last tuft of whitish hollow hair scattered by the wind.

With the passage of each day, the pups demanded more of the female's rich milk, and though the morsels that the pack returned with were welcome and sought after, the gray bitch needed more. During the first week, she had stayed within a few hundred yards of the den, her ears tuned to the small tremblings of sound which traveled from below ground. At first, she had been on her feet instantly to disappear into the den, where, at the least, she would quickly assure herself that her pups were still there in the darkness. This almost feverish attention served little practical purpose, and had only helped thin her already emaciated body further. Then her concern slowly lessened and she became more selective when motivated to make the trip down the long passageway. Finally, during the late afternoon of the seventh day, she left the den trotting easily at the black male's side as the pack dropped into the ravine below the den meadow. Her nervousness had given way to a more basic need, a need for food in abundant quantity.

The wolves trotted leisurely, separating and then rejoining in an apparently random manner, as they followed an ancient sheep trail which meandered across the face of the lower slopes. Cut into the punky turf, an undulating slash in the carpetlike ground willow, the trail offered an easy, if not direct, route of travel to the east. It was but one of many that formed a network followed by each successive generation of the white Dall sheep that lived out their short lives in this part of the range.

Higher, among the ridges and peaks of the mountains, such trails disappeared, visible only where they crossed patches of lichens which grew carpetlike in the high passes. Only the sheep seemed to know where these obscure interconnections in the network were, and they followed them unerringly.

The trail took the pack downward to a point only a few hundred feet above the top edge of a spruce-choked draw where it merged with the gravel outfall of an ancient rocky bluff. The promontory was steep, and at its foot was a naturally occurring salt lick. Here, during the early spring and autumn, sheep dug at the russet saline soil and consumed it, along with small pebbles which popped between their yellow teeth. The sheep craved the salt and needed it, but the wolves seemed unaware of its presence. The lick was vacant, however, the lambing season having already started, and the small band of pregnant ewes that visited briefly more than a week before had moved into the higher country to bear their young.

The wolves worked their way downward and across a tilted field of broken rock and gravel, moving slowly and savoring the rich musk that saturated the ground. Even when the ground was frozen hard during late autumn and blown free of snow during winter, it was a place that the black male liked to visit. On many occasions he had perpetrated upon his followers side trips consisting of many miles just to indulge his senses with the scent left by the sheep. Scatterings of black, beanlike droppings and the pungent urine made for a heady experience which invariably ended in his rolling luxuriously, sending cascades of gravel streaming downward to the wash's foot.

For the sheep, the annual migration to the lambing meadows was an event which seemed to provide the greatest degree of safety during a time when the flocks were most vulnerable. Then, as summer matured, they would move even higher among the chimneyed rocks. Finally, with the snow of another winter covering the ground willow and other plants upon which they depended, the bands would be pushed invariably downward once more. Their return to browse among taller willows which protruded through deep snow in the low valleys would once more place them within reach of the wolves.

The bands of pregnant ewes were most uniform in their composition, the rams, both young and old, having withdrawn and secluded themselves among the rocky chimneys and high ravines. Here they were content to rest while building and storing a layer of hard, white tallow.

The tiny, spindle-legged lambs would be born in early June, to begin feeding precociously on native vegetation when only a few hours old. If there is an idyllic existence among the creatures of the Arctic, it must be that of the Dall sheep, but as the wolves passed the lick, only their scent which clung to the rocks of the salt lick told of their presence in the mountains. Satisfied, the black leader resumed his trotting gait as he slipped downward to rejoin the rest of the pack.

Later, and still traveling with little apparent purpose, the wolves emerged upon a sedge-covered plateau. The ground here was wet and soft, the thaw having produced standing pools of shallow water which were already well hidden by a mat of growing vegetation. A broken line of spindly spruce bordered its lower edge where the terrain once more dropped gently to merge with the flats beyond.

Slightly less than fifteen miles had been covered by the wolves before they rested among the willows and grass, which already reached their shoulders. Sitting on her haunches and panting with the effort of travel, the gray bitch felt the wind with her nose as it freshened from the east. With the absence of the sun it was cool and she shivered involuntarily while watching her towering mate as he cropped shoots of sprouting bear grass, then coughed them up along with phlegm from his throat. The ritual served some little-understood purpose, and was one which all of the wolves engaged in frequently during spring and early summer. Perhaps the green shoots provided a needed nutrient or, more simply, the coughing regurgitation produced by the barblike hairs of the grass blades purged the consumer of at least some of the stomach worms that each wolf carried.

The sky, which had been cloudless during the afternoon and early evening, had become overcast, and gray curtains of misty rain hung like great tapestries which obscured the western horizon. Below the vantage point shared by the wolves, a series of ponds turned to dull metal as the vagrant wind roughened their surfaces; then they regained the mirrorlike sheen which reflected the dull sky as the gusts passed.

Along the foot of the mountains were thousands of such shallow ponds. Formed by seeps in the countless moraine pockets, they were bordered by willows, made lush in the presence of standing water, and a few gnarled spruce. The ponds were virtually devoid of the aquatic life found in warmer waters at lower elevations. While serving as breeding receptacles for hordes of mosquitoes which numbered in the countless millions, such ponds varied in size from a few square feet to a half mile or more in diameter, the larger attracting occasional pairs of nesting scaup and bufflehead ducks. Even the old squaw, a sea duck by nature, was an occasional visitor here, and during spring the males were still resplendent in the white patches and long recurved tails of breeding plumage.

Because they were shallow and largely supplied by seeping ground water during the warm months, such ponds often froze to their bottoms during the winter and, as a result, seldom bore more than token bottom vegetation. For this reason, even the moose that bred here during the autumn rut shunned them except as a place to drink and escape the lingering insects during the occasional warm days of late September.

Suddenly the black male was on his feet. He had grown restless for reasons that were not obvious, and trotted haltingly along the bent grass that marked his back trail. Stopping, he snuffled among the wet sedges before returning to the gray bitch's side, his tail held high. Then, raising his muzzle, he stood on his hind legs, testing the erratically moving air, after which he glided quickly to the lower edge of the plateau-like meadow. The gray bitch followed a short distance behind, caught up in a mild, but as yet undefined, excitement. Then, stopping abruptly, she watched a V-shaped wake of rippling water which was slowly dividing the largest of the ponds below.

The beaver had lived here for half a decade, and weighed more than forty pounds. His purpose on the pond was seemingly an erratic exercise in simple pleasure after a long winter spent sealed in a world of faint blue light beneath the ice and the total darkness of the lodge that stood adjacent to the pond's trickling outlet. The dome-shaped structure weighed several tons, and was an old one, having been occupied by numerous generations of the spade-tailed animals even before its current residents had arrived five summers earlier. It was prominent on the pond, and marked the epicenter of the small territory claimed by the beaver and his lifelong mate. Thatched with willow branches and cemented with pond mud, the lodge stood six feet above the water's normal level, below which it connected to the pond's shore.

The structure's usefulness as a dwelling place was predicated solely upon the level of the pond. Low on its perimeter and submerged was the lodge's only entrance, its location the result of instinctive planning by its first occupants and builders. It effectively screened intruders, and only the nervously efficient muskrats which frequented the pond entered here, along with an occasional mink. The beavers coexisted with the former and promptly evicted the latter.

The big chestnut-furred male and his mate had spent each successive season raising young here, then forcing them out to fend for themselves during the second spring following their birth. Seldom had their numerous offspring become established in other ponds, however, for there were few ponds that were large enough or deep enough, and in their travels they had regularly fallen prey to lynx, wolverines, and wolves. Their sacrifice had served little obvious purpose except to assure their parents of a competition-free environment, which left more of the slippery sweet aspen bark to be found along the margin of this pond and others nearby.

Even with the pond's minimal population thus neatly arranged, the willows which once stood in taller profusion around its perimeter had been thinned at an alarming rate. They would, therefore, cease to support even one pair of beaver before the decade passed. As a result, even if a future pair of wandering two-year-olds were to happen upon the still usable lodge, they would shun it to look elsewhere for a home.

The gray bitch was already working toward the pond, followed by her black mate. Though she had not yet identified the diverging wake left by the swimming beaver, experience told her that the movement pattern was not caused by the wind. No sound had accompanied the discovery, and the breeze was wrong for purposes of cross-checking with her nose, though she tried repeatedly. The other pack members had not yet been alerted, but the two buff males followed their father through simple habit.

As the wolves descended the gradual slope beneath the tundra bench, the two white females lagged behind, and in the half-light filtering through the misty rain which had begun to fall the white wolves stood out in stark relief against the dark vegetation on the hillside. Their slightest movement could have been spotted instantly by any animal that made a business of watching for wolves, but the beaver was apparently attuned only to his contented boredom as he alternately nipped the succulent lower branches of a willow bush and preened his fine pelt with the specially split nails on one of the toes of each hind foot. While preening his fur, he transferred an oily secretion called castoreum from glands beneath the base of his scaled tail, thus partially waterproofing his pelt.

When the beaver and his mate had moved in here they had found the pond's outlet only partially checked, and they had begun to rebuild the dam during the first night. Finally, after several days of unceasing effort, the flow was stanched enough to cause the water level in the pond to gradually rise almost two feet, thus hiding the entrance tunnel. The seasons which had passed since that time were then spent in obsessed instinctive devotion to the never-ending task of repairing holes where washouts occurred and muskrats had stolen from the dam's content.

That the pair had lived here relatively undisturbed was more the result of coincidence than preplanning. Even dur-

ing midwinter the St. George Creek pack had visited the
lodge to sniff the frost encrustations where small air leaks
exited. At such times, the faint sounds of digging would
have reached the beavers' ears had they not been drifting in
the idle sleep of semidormancy. Even had they noticed the
sounds from above there would have been little cause for
alarm, for the concrete texture of the domed lodge was im-
pervious to all efforts to penetrate it. Because of such security, both instinctive and coincidental, the beavers had
grown accustomed to an almost tranquil existence.

The male beaver's presence on the pond was, however,
more than a coincidence. Recently, three blunt-nosed, half-
blind kits had been born in the velvet darkness of the
lodge's nest chamber, and the female had forced him out
into the open. He had accepted this eviction as he had during springs past and, as a result, had spent the past three
days cruising on and beneath the pond's surface, dozing for
short periods while afloat in the shallow water opposite the
lodge, and feeding silently among the willows that bordered
the pond. He had accomplished little but remained serenely
happy with his lot.

Somewhere on an adjacent pond, a shorebird piped
thinly, the plaintive sound carrying on a vagrant wind gust.
Less than a hundred yards separated the beaver from the
wolves, and the gray bitch flattened her ears as the cool
musky scent finally ran into her dilating nostrils. The pair
was closer to the pond's edge than were their buff-colored
sons, but due to a shift and lull in the breeze, all four of the
wolves were now guided by the ribbon of scent that flowed
and ebbed above the top of the wet grass. Though they
moved toward the same goal, each was pulled by his or her
own nose, and only when one of them initiated the final rush
would the chase become a visual exercise. Finally, and as if
on signal, the stalking wolves flattened themselves in the

nodding sedges, the only movement their slowly wagging tails.

As he swam once more, the special valves in the beaver's mouth and tiny cup-shaped ears closed as he submerged, and his broadly webbed hind feet propelled him smoothly ahead of the plumes of silt his passage raised along the pond's floor. Because of his oversized lungs and liver used to store the oxygen he breathed, if he so desired, he could have stayed submerged for a quarter hour, but seldom did. His finely furred chestnut pelt appeared to be bathed in oil as he swam a slow circle after surfacing once more. The droplets of cold rain that dimpled the pond's surface made no impression upon him, and pulling himself out onto a gravel spit, he turned to face the water and stare myopically for several minutes in the direction of the lodge.

Though the beaver had grown old by the standards of his race, his teeth had not. Unlike other bone tissue, the two-inch incisors had grown constantly throughout his lifetime, kept continuously sharp with constant cutting of woody plants. Without such use, the massive orange-colored teeth would have quickly begun to grow out of control, eventually becoming functionless even as tools for survival, which might have resulted in one of nature's most macabre deaths as the lengthening teeth slowly killed their owner by growing inexorably upward through the roof of his mouth to finally penetrate his small brain.

In his frequent travels, the beaver had left his sign in obvious disarray. Near the pond, wide paths of matted grass extended away from the water's edge, and the shore itself was littered with branch cuttings. Green leaves floated on the surface of the pond where they had been cut or broken from clusters of small limbs held tightly against the muscular chest as he swam.

Such cutting and hauling would continue until the pond froze once more, and this served two major purposes. Some of the green branches were packed into the small places in the dam, but most were simply shoved into the mud at the dam's base and, more often, at the submerged perimeter of the lodge. Such cuttings, preserved by the low temperature of the pond's water, would feed the colony during the long winter ahead.

Scent is a fickle quantity, but one which the gray wolf relies upon as the basis for life. It exists, in greater or lesser quantity, as submicroscopic airborne moisture particles that are detectable by the nose and interpreted by the brain. So sensitive is the broad nose of the wolf that the direction taken by a passing snowshoe hare even on a dry subzero day can be appraised almost instantly, well after the fact. The wet earthy smell of a beaver, enriched by the sweetish castor secreted by glands near his anus, provided both the gray bitch and the black leader with a sensory pathway to the pond's shore that was only mildly confusing due to its potency.

Though the gray bitch was the first to locate the beaver's sign on the pond's surface, she accepted directional clues from her mate during the stalk, thereby relinquishing leadership to the big black. Though the position he occupied in the pack hierarchy demanded it, it was not an act of aggressive competition as much as an exercise in automatic cooperation, the employment of which was unquestioned. Were it not so, the concept of the pack would have been a useless one. In this hierarchy, the old bitch was second only to her mate, and were he to be lost, the priority of such leadership would probably become hers alone, as a result of habit patterns sustained and honed during the passage of twenty million years.

It was a result of this same system that had caused the white resident bitches to remain above the stalking wolves. Not only were they the lowest members in the social order of the pack and strongly subservient to the old gray bitch, they were simply inexperienced hunters. The two factors made them spectators to the events occurring below them and near the pond.

No movement met the leader's eyes as he slowly raised his broad head above the whispering grass. The wind had gained velocity as a passing squall turned the undersides of new leaves to silver; and crouched low, he had swung with it instinctively. The gray bitch had followed at his hip, and the new course which they followed had led them downwind from the scent source, giving it new strength and more positive direction.

As he worked on a sapling he had felled the night before, the soft clicking and sodden scraping sounds made by the beaver's teeth attested to the power his jaw exerted. They were sounds to which he had spent his lifetime growing accustomed, and as such they required no concealment. They were, however, magnified in his ears by the bone structure of his skull, and masked his ordinarily good sense of hearing, but five million years of evolution in a world of aquatic safety had made him careless. As a result, like the wetly vibrant sounds caused by the pressure changes which occurred each time he submerged, he was not aware of them.

Had the beaver remained in the water, he would have become only the object of curious observation on the part of the wolves. Away from the pond's protection, however, he instantly became a highly desirable and accessible meal.

The gray bitch heard the soft sounds of the beaver's teeth, and still belly-crawling, she once more froze. Her black mate glanced back over his shoulder, and followed suit. The short pathway to the object of their intense search had now become clearly marked and impossible to lose.

Instants later, tail down and running low to the ground, the pack leader's blurred rush carried him past the beaver. To compensate for his mistake, he leaped high, somersaulting over himself and turning in midair. The gray bitch had been more fortunate, and her teeth locked in the powerful mass of muscle tissue at the base of the beaver's skull. Her own final fifteen-foot bound tumbled both herself and her prey into a rain-saturated clump of red-barked willow.

The beaver's stolid nature, the false sense of security that his world of water had seemed to provide, and the quiet sounds of his eating had, in reality, been mere subfactors in his death. The real cause was far less obvious, and stemmed directly from the disappearing supply of food that the pond still offered. This year he had found that he had to travel farther than ever before to find willows unstunted by previous cutting. As a result, when the abrupt end to his life came, he was much farther from the safety of the pond than he should have been.

The leader's aborted leap had caused an interruption that lasted less than a full second, and even before the gray bitch lunged to twist her body into a position which straddled the beaver, the leader had taken a deep hold on the beaver's compact hind quarter. His belated help served to hold the powerful animal, which was already kicking violently, its neck crushed between the bitch's jaws. The adrenaline surge of castor musk caused both wolves to work their teeth deeper and hold on even after the beaver was dead.

The stilt-legged shorebird screamed again as it lifted haltingly into the wind, and the sound broke the silence that had attended the stalk and kill. The meal which followed was completed quickly and with little ceremony, the gray bitch gulping more than the amount that would have, under other circumstances, comprised her share. The buff males consumed the small bones and entrails, leaving only part of the shredded hide still attached to the furred skull, which the gray bitch carried to a place well away from the pond and buried quickly in the soft mud.

For the old female, the stalk, kill, and eventual meal of

dark purplish meat was a powerful stimulus after weeks of waning activity near the den. The kill, however, was routine and of little importance to the long-term well-being of the St. George Creek pack. It had required less than half an hour to accomplish. Though the old wolf panted audibly, her breath condensing in the damp air, she rested only briefly with the black and her adult sons. Then, rising, she shook the rain from her matted coat, and without hesitation trotted rapidly upslope toward the rain-shrouded mountains. One of the buff males followed while the other stayed with the black leader near the pond.

Compelled by a quick desire to feel the warmth of her pups and to regain the quiet darkness of the den, she began the homeward trip, accompanied by her son and followed at a distance by the two white wolves, who would later deviate from the direct route to spend several hours mousing near the remains of an abandoned miner's shack near the mouth of Friday Creek. Her mate dallied near the pond until the sky began to lighten once more before swinging farther east and finally circling back to the salt lick. Here he initiated his son in the delights of rolling in a thin skin of reddish, scent-saturated mud before returning to the St. George Creek den.

CHAPTER 5

With the arrival of the final week in June, and the passage of the summer solstice, warm twenty-four-hour daylight flooded the lush flats and carpeted foothills of the Alaska Range. Though the higher peaks retained the snow of many winters as the sun traced its slow path above the horizon during the long days, the lesser peaks darkened with the advanced thaw. With June's three-quarter mark, the shortening of each passing day would begin once more, eventually taking a full ten minutes of light from each until, by midwinter, almost full darkness would once again cloak the frozen land throughout each long day. For now, however, the high Arctic sun slipped below the far horizon for only a few hours each night, producing a prolonged twilight during which the air cooled slightly and the gusting wind subsided.

It was a time of movement. New aspen leaves, glossy with a waxy coating that perfumed the air, tumbled before the wind, giving the trees the appearance of meadow grass. Willows flashed silver as the warm wind exposed the undersides of lance-shaped leaves, and the dark spruce swayed, their branches soft with the light-green tufts of new needles and immature cones.

Along the bigger rivers, during midday, clouds of tan,

wind-roiled silt rode over the dark water. No rain had fallen since the night of the beaver kill, and St. George Creek had shriveled to an unimpressive trickle. Dust devils swirled and marched along the creek bottom, and paper wasps built their small cocoonlike hives beneath rock overhangs. The pack slept away the long, sometimes hot daylight hours, moving from loafing places beneath the shaded ledges along the upper edge of the den meadow only to drink frequently of the creek water.

Even the grizzly bear that had taken up temporary residence where the creek tumbled onto the flats below the St. George Creek drainage dozed through most of each day. As he stretched ludicrously on his thinly furred belly among the willow clumps, dappled leaf shadows marched and retreated across his broad rump and back, and he grunted softly, absorbing the slight coolness the damp ground afforded.

The bear was blond, his hide dull with the rolling he had done in the reddish tundra dust since emerging from his long sleep the winter before. He bore a dark-colored hairless patch on his right hip, a rubbed spot that contrasted sharply with the short honey-colored pelt that covered the rest of his three-hundred-pound body. A four-year-old male, he had become a regular along the lower slopes that were traveled by the St. George Creek pack when it left the home valley to hunt. The wolves paid scant attention to his presence, however, and a state of armed truce seemed to prevail.

The black leader often paused during the pack's frequent passages to watch the shuffling grizzly as he poked among the vegetation of the willow fringes for the yellow, tuberous roots of wild peavine. At such times, the punky sounds of his digging carried clearly to the big wolf, and seemed to fascinate him even more than the bear itself.

A vegetarian by choice during the late spring and summer, the grizzly had not killed since he left the small, rock-lined chamber above McCamber Creek, where he had slept through the last two winters. Because of his penchant for the starchy rootstocks of peavine and willow, the spaces between his massive brown-stained molars had become tightly packed with bark and other fibrous debris. The small advantage produced as the coarse food partially cleaned his teeth would be overshadowed in coming years by the formation of festering abscesses that would add to the general discomfort of passing from maturity to old age and finally senility. The few parka squirrels that he had managed to exhume from the countless dens that perforated the slopes had provided amusement but scant nourishment. They were difficult to catch, and the bear's ivory-tipped claws had moved as much as a ton of earth on given afternoons to be rewarded only with the blunting wear they received. He was, if nothing else, an inveterate optimist.

In the recent past, the grizzly had sought out a sow and mated with her only after killing the pair of cubs that had been born during her own semihibernation of the winter before. Though the sow, smaller and darker colored than the boar, had raked him with her claws while protecting her twins, it had been a futile endeavor. A week had been required for both adults to forget, after which they coupled, and then went their separate ways.

The boar was not only an optimist but an opportunist as well. As he slept in the shade, habit dictated that he face downhill. At such times he was invisible among the short willows, the only movement being that produced by the wind as it winnowed the long hairs on his shoulders and back and the frequent dilation of his nostrils as he tested the breeze. From his position in the moving shadows he could launch a silent, side-winding rush downslope and, with luck, overwhelm a passing caribou. The animals were scarce, however, and their absence, along with prodigious quantities of willow roots he had consumed, dulled his desire to hunt.

During the early spring, when he awakened from six months of semidormant sleep, both his stomach and disposition had been sour. Into this, his fourth spring of life, he had once more emerged to find the land streaked with snow and offering little nourishment. He was thin, but his winter coat had been luxurious and glossy, and it rippled as he shuffled along the still-frozen trails leading downward toward the flats. He sought the nourishment-weak new vegetation, among which he bore an unexplained preference for the gritty horsetail fern. The lacy prehistoric plant contained minute particles of sandy silica, which may have performed an abrasive function as it passed through his digestive tract. The purging of his flaccid belly took more than three weeks to complete, and though it sweetened his sleep-fouled breath, it did little to improve his attitude toward his surroundings and those with which he shared them.

The bear was only vaguely aware of the wolves' presence in his territory. He had noticed their scent as it washed through the gullies that he frequented, but he had seen them infrequently. Though the pack had often passed closely as he fed, his myopic vision yielded only gray blurs, and on such occasions he swung his broad head in the direction from which the canine scent flowed before returning to whatever business occupied his attention at the time. The black wolf seldom closed the distance between the bear and himself to less than a few hundred yards. For the buff males, however, the grizzly had on certain occasions provided a dangerous diversion.

The game consisted of harassment, and the two males called the tune by barking and nipping at the boar's heels as he sought only to move away from his quick-footed tormentors. The black had watched from a distance, his tail wagging in apparent amusement, as the buff wolves finally incited the chase from which they had always emerged victors. Only their eventual boredom allowed the shuffling bear to go his solitary way as the wolves moved on to other places.

Where once the gray bitch's pups responded only to the soft earth virbrations that pulsed to them upon her return to the den, they quickly became proficient at catching her warm scent as she entered and descended the den tunnel. Hers was the first scent to be catalogued in their memories, one which would dominate all others during the entirety of their lives. As the warm musk of the lactating bitch became increasingly distinguishable among the other earthy odors of the den, its surging presence sparked the imprint that would cornerstone the development of a social pattern that sets wolves apart from all other Alaskan predators. Because of this process, the bitch's scent and its presence guaranteed the rapid formation of a well from which all of the pups' developing habit patterns would spring.

After eleven days their eyes had begun to open, the lids separating by varying degrees to reveal milky blue glints in the postnatal blandness of puny faces. With sight developing, the pups quickly gained the ability to orient themselves, and as their eyelids separated fully they began to make feeble attempts to stand in the gloom of the den chamber. Perhaps most important, they found the sources of scent that their noses had already detected easier to locate.

During their third week, the last of the three basic senses which had lain dormant since birth began to take form, but so gradually that it produced little obvious change in the pups' behavior. The capacity to hear was, however, the motivation which caused the little female pup to seek the mouth of the den.

It was a long and tiring trip, one which was finally completed only after a number of false starts. With her ratty tail tucked tightly between her legs, the little wolf emerged into blinding sunlight, where she resisted the temptation to flee only because of the nearness of the bitch. As the old female licked the wobbly pup vigorously, she was joined by her black mate and one of her buff-colored sons. The pup's emergence was then celebrated by wagging tails and tongue lolling, but she was still too frightened and stunned by the sun's warmth and brilliance to notice.

Later that same afternoon, she ventured to the surface once more, this time accompanied by the rest of the litter. The gray bitch welcomed them as avidly as she had when they first emerged from her own body, and her closeness further cemented the bond between the litter and herself, a bond that was already vital and unbreakable.

It has been said that a wolf is not a wolf until it is an adult, and there is some truth to the adage, for more than any other animal in the Arctic, wolves are a product of their rearing. Even as the four potbellied pups stood tail-hung and blinking in the white sun while somehow resisting the temptation to flee into the familiar coolness of the den, they had already crossed the first of countless chasms that would finally see them through their adolescence, a period of two years during which they would face all of the harsh and potentially destructive forces that adult wolves fall heir to.

Time passed swiftly following the emergence of the pups from the den. Summer matured unnoticed, and by mid-July their body weights had increased almost tenfold. The first two months following whelping had been a period during which growth had rapidly taken place. One of the pups, a male, quickly outstripped his littermates in size, weighing a full fifteen pounds more. The other two males were his mirror image though slightly smaller. All three of the male pups bore the dark, smoky coloration of their sire.

The female differed from her brothers in two ways, both obvious. She was a runt, and the thin fine-textured hair that covered her body was light gray, almost ivory. This latter characteristic was a genetic variance which rarely occurred in litters sired by the gray bitch's black mate, and all of her previous pups had, without exception, borne some variation of his dark color.

The phenomenal growth which lengthened legs, strengthened sinews and ligaments, gradually closed bone sutures, and absorbed the sagging bellies of early puphood continued seemingly unabated even after weaning, which was accomplished during mid-July. The change in diet from the supply of rich milk was a gradual one, hurried by physiological processes and the growing tenderness of the gray bitch's pendulous breasts.

During the early weeks she had allowed the pups unlimited access to the supply of yellow milk she produced, a supply more than adequate for the small litter. Then, as the pups grew stronger, and the nursing habit often overrode their actual need for food, she grew almost defensive in her attitude toward them. She began to leave the pups to their own devices for increasing periods of time, until finally their needle-sharp teeth and incessant bunting had told her that the time for them to begin eating solid food was at hand.

The four pups quickly learned to eat what the gray bitch ate. The change from her milk to meat was more than a mere dietary adjustment, however. It was a process that involved not only the gray bitch but most other members of the pack. As such it further established a bond between the pups and their huge sire, a bond which had been formed during his frequent visits to the subterranean den chamber during their first two weeks of life.

Returning from the hunt, the black wolf would immediately accompany the waiting bitch to the mouth of the den. His arrival there soon became an anticipated signal to the four pups that the time to eat was at hand. At first, the black disgorged several pounds of bright-red, coarsely chewed meat without coaxing from the pups. They quickly learned to consume the meat, which was as fresh and unaffected by his own digestive juices as it had been when the big male had stripped it from the carcass of the animal that had provided it.

On frequent occasions, the buff-colored wolves stayed behind as the rest of the pack left the meadow to hunt. Somewhat incongruously, they seemed to enjoy the chore of watching over the gray bitch's pups, romping with them often during the warm days, and when not engaged in play, lying idle, dozing nearby in the sun but always alert to the pups' presence.

These domestic tasks, like the feeding of the pups that had quickly become a responsibility shared by the big leader, and even the growing willingness of the standoffish resident bitches to play with the pups, seemed to overshadow more rigid adherence to social discipline and the recognition of individual status among the pack members. Though this slackening of protocol would pass with the fleeting weeks of early summer, for now it stood as yet one more proof of the success that the pack concept seems to guarantee.

As the process of weaning continued, the pups soon learned, through repetition, to sense the pack's return, and took to waiting patiently at the den mouth. Then later, as the adults entered the St. George Creek meadow, they ran to meet them, frolicking beneath the chest and muzzle of not only the black male but the others as well. Standing on their hind legs, they mouthed the throats and muzzles of the adults to stimulate the disgorging habit and make food available as quickly as possible. Then, as the gray bitch began to accompany the rest of the pack on hunting expeditions, she became the first of the wolves to receive the attention of her pups upon their return.

As the pups grew, other physical changes beyond their in-

creasing size became apparent. The snipped muzzles and
wrinkled faces with which they had been born were gradually replaced by more wolf-like appearances. Though at two
months their ears were still too large, the pups' legs and
muzzles had lengthened noticeably, and in the sometimes
stifling heat of early August, their long tongues panted with
the exertion of play.

For the pups, fatigue seemed to be an unknown quantity,
or at least one which could be neutralized by a short nap
whenever the urge was felt. The feeble lunges of early
puppyhood rapidly became short dashes of adolescence.
These, in turn, quickly became full-blown circling races
which required most of the space afforded by the den
meadow.

At first, such romps involved only the four pups. They
were soon joined, however, by the black pack leader, who
seemingly shed his dominant role to playfully engage in an
agile imitation of the pups' antics. Even the two resident females tagged behind, wagging their plumed tails in vicari-
ous enjoyment, but always reluctant to join in. Unexplaina-
bly, the gray bitch usually remained apart during these play
sessions, seemingly content to watch from some vantage
point nearby.

With further growth and added strength, the random
tumbling and running that had consumed most of the pups'
waking hours became more sophisticated, while gaining direction and purpose. With time, play became mock combat,
and the pups were once again left to their own devices by
the adults of the pack. At first, serious fights were rare, ter-
minating with the first sharp yelp elicited by a pinched lip
or ear. At such times, the victim of exaggerated pain usually
left the group to sulk, and to be quickly joined by nearby
adult members of the pack.

With the arrival of mid-August, the violet-colored fireweed which grew in distant profusion on the flats below the

slopes had darkened in hue. The pups now worked as a team as they destroyed tussocks of grass, small gravel piles, butterflies, and the dwarf willows that already showed the red-colored leaves that would carpet the slopes with almost monotonous brilliance during early autumn. The pups had actually learned little since their birth except to revel in the exhilaration of running. Subtle changes had, however, taken place, but they came as a result of the competition of violent physical exercise rather than through formal lessons. Nonetheless, reflexes became sharper as the rudiments of learned behavior slowly replaced the less orderly expenditure of early puppyhood energy.

The gray bitch's pups accepted the den meadow boundaries as the edge of their known world. The den itself, however, became less important to them as the summer days shortened imperceptibly. Where once it was the epicenter from which they had sprung, to be returned to as a sanctuary from hunger, pain, loneliness, and all of the other seemingly crushing experiences that puppies experience, it was now used infrequently.

As they entered the third month of their lives, the pups knew each hole, ledge, and fissure in the meadow's surface as well as they had known the dark interior of the den chamber. The place held nothing new for them, yet they somehow sustained an interest in each tuft of wind-flattened willow, and every raven that swooped down upon them in mock attack as they played. Their world was small but basically comfortable, while lending a sort of stability to the one brief period in their lives that closely approached total security. Then, with the arrival of mid-August, even this changed abruptly.

❧ CHAPTER 6

After a few days of cool weather it once more turned hot, and a buzzing paper wasp hovered over the sleeping bitch's head, then dropped boldly to within a few inches of her muzzle. With a lightning snap she ended its life and rolled the insect on her tongue before swallowing it. One of the male pups had already been stung painfully, then spent the following night in misery as he licked the hard, knotlike swelling on his naked, soft-skinned abdomen. With the cooling nights and shortening days of late summer, insect life had become strangely plentiful among the benchlike foothills of the mountains. It seemed to be a time for swarming and congregation, and along with bees and wasps, yellow clouds of sulphur butterflies clustered on spots of dampness in the sand and gravel that bordered St. George Creek.

Lying on her side in the scant shade afforded by the slight overhang above the den mouth, the gray bitch sniffed the warm air, which had become heavy with the smell of smoke, and her lolling tongue accentuated the heaving of her flanks. The pack had returned to the den meadow during midmorning after one of its frequent forays onto the muskeg-laced flats below. Even there, as they drifted among the dark spruces, the air had not been cool, and the scent of pitch liquefying under the effect of the early sun masked

more subtle odors that ran along the dry moss of the forest
floor.

Raising her head slowly, the bitch tested the slow-moving
air currents that wafted upslope from the southwest, and
watched a pair of bald eagles partially obscured in haze as
they circled high overhead on motionless wings. The smoke
that the almost unnoticeable breeze carried was far from a
new experience for the old wolf. It was, in fact, one which
she had experienced during each summer of her long life,
though the wildfires that produced it remained unknown to
her.

This fire had burned with little change in direction for almost three weeks, and had already incinerated more than
250,000 acres of wilderness. Its front, an orange wall of
crackling flame under dark plumes of smoke, moved at the
astonishing rate of almost five miles each day, perpetuating
the fire and providing it with fresh fuel. Ahead of it, sometimes a fourth of a mile, new fires leaped into being, the result of spontaneous combustion. The fire was not, however,
a threat to the St. George Creek wolves, for it burned over
two hundred miles west of the pack's extensive range.

Like dozens of others, large and small, the fire had been
ignited by lightning during a summer storm, and though ap-
palling in its evil appearance and devastating nature, it
would produce subtle benefits that were far from obvious in
the plain of snowlike ash that it left in its wake.

It burned in a valley similar to that which contained the
Tanana River, though smaller and more narrowly confined.
The dense spruce stands of its floor and bordering slopes
had caught the brunt of its awesome wind-generated heat,
and since its birth the fire had made repeated advances toward the tops of the ridges which defined the valley. Also,
like the Tanana Flats, the floor of the burning valley was an
area where moose had become scarce, not because of the
inroads of man or hunting wolves, but simply because the

vegetation which it once supported had grown out of reach of, or already nipped back by, the great browsers.

Aspen stands which had once been a mere ten feet tall had matured, rapidly outstripping the growth rate of almost all other woody vegetation. Where once the countless gravel bars along the valley's rivers supported dense stands of willows, however, only a sea of blunt stubs had existed before the fire, attesting to heavy feeding during many winters by a once-dense local population of moose.

As a result, and long before fire swept the land, the valley had become virtually useless as a dependably adequate and accessible food supply for the seven-foot-tall ruminants, each of which required almost fifty pounds of fresh vegetation per day. The incineration of their range would eventually regenerate the valley's original value as a supplier of food. After only a year, fireweed would flourish in the vast openings produced by the fire, and with the passage of a few seasons more, aspen and other willow species would invade the spaces among the blackened trunks and snags. It would, as a result, slowly become attractive once more and moose would move back into the feeding grounds once used by their forebears. That such moose would be followed closely by wolves would be the signal that the land had once more come full cycle.

The gray bitch's pups paid scant notice to the smoky scent and bluish cast which tainted the early August air over the den meadow. They still gamboled tirelessly under the high sun, swooping down at frequent intervals to harass the bitch as she sought sleep. She snapped at them as they passed, but with little real enthusiasm, and during her frequent trips to the trickling water that remained in St. George Creek they accompanied her to mimic her drinking.

During recent days the pups had followed the gray bitch and her mate into the confines of the creek gully below the den meadow. They had been reluctant to do so, however, and upon several occasions they had turned back, returning to the drainage's mouth, where they set up an incessant yapping.

The long afternoon hours passed slowly, and as the gray bitch drowsed, a wall of cloud moved slowly over the flats from the southwest. Its leading edge quickly plunged the distant horizon into smoke-stained shadow, seemingly detaching it from the land itself. Though the sun still bathed the den meadow, the air was cooling noticeably, and the old wolf rolled to a standing position to shake the red dust from her coat and to stretch the cramped muscles of her hips and gimped hind leg.

The breeze now carried the faint scent of rain as the four pups charged uphill in a spontaneous mock attack upon one of the resident females. Rising from his concealed place among the short willows of the rock-strewn creekbed, the black sat to rub the encrustations of insect welts on his muzzle and then, after biting halfheartedly at his upper foreleg, trotted slowly uphill to butt the gray bitch with his broad forehead.

As if by prearranged plan, the pack then joined up at the den mouth, clustering around the gray bitch with wagging tails. The pups played among the legs of the adults as the black wolf scratched once more, then stood to move slowly downslope. The pack followed him in line as he entered the rocky gully that led to the flats. This time the pups did not turn back.

The pack moved slowly downward and out onto the gradual slopes below the St. George Creek drainage, stopping often to disperse and make short excursions among the hanging ledges and boulders. During these side trips, the pups shouldered each other in their efforts to stay close to the gray bitch, for though they had spent the entirety of their short lives less than a mile away they were nervous. The sun left the slopes quickly, plunging them into deep shadow as the pack turned south following a familiar trail which snaked invisibly among the scarlet dwarf willow and brownish moss.

Following the two buff males, the black leader watched them swing downslope where the soft sponginess of moss gave way to loose gravel spills scattered among brackish seeps. It was a route which the wolves had used little during the summer months, one which would take them northward and onto the flats. Gradually becoming comfortable with their new and rapidly changing surroundings, the pups reverted to their usual tumbling play, crowding the gray bitch as the gloom of the spruces swallowed the moving pack.

The wolves moved silently and with more purpose as the black, leading again, threaded his way through an intricate network of deep-cut moose trails, his passage marked only by the occasional clucking of red squirrels. The wolves were soon well away from the foot of the slopes that flanked the mountains, and the range's white peaks were framed only occasionally behind the lattice of dark spruce. Beneath the conifers, year-round shadow had effectively stunted or prohibited the growth of underbrush, and the traveling was easy. Several miles slipped by quickly, after which the pack moved out onto a broad meadow of saw grass already coated with evening dew and studded heavily with barkless down timber and bleached, upturned roots. It was a place which during some unremembered season past had suffered the ravages of a violent windstorm, and it was a place that the St. George Creek pack knew well.

For some reason, the broad secluded meadow, along with certain others almost identical to it, had been selected by wolves during past generations as temporary gathering or nursing places. The meadows were no different in outward appearance from countless others, yet the gray bitch had returned to them during each autumn to deposit her pups while she hunted elsewhere with the pack.

The wolves' arrival on the nursery meadow occurred just after midnight, and the clearing lay silent under a quarter-moon, which appeared for brief periods through gathering clouds. It had not rained during the day, though a brief storm had moved across the far end of the vast flats, and only a chill gusting wind had evidenced its nearness. The air over the meadow was calm, and a dampness which settled out as dew on the dry grass whitened it in the weak light.

The pack lingered on the meadow during the following day, resting in the cool darkness of the grassy tunnels before leaving as a unit to hunt. The four pups had an opportunity to familiarize themselves with their new surroundings, exploring among the dead root snags and fallen timber. Voles, mice, and shrews were plentiful in the thick saw grass of the meadow, and by imitation they quickly learned to locate, if not catch, the tiny rodents. Even the adults made a game of it, often leaping high in the air over a scurrying red-backed vole, then pouncing to pin it down with their paws.

During the final days of August, the nights had begun to grow cold, and layers of heavy ground fog settled over the meadow. Autumn had quickly become a tangible thing, to be smelled in the musky scent of highbush cranberry and dying leaves that already layered and decayed in the shallow water at the edges of stagnant ponds and other wet places. The approach of another long winter was evident too in the cuttings of beaver colonies that occupied the bigger sloughs and provided the wolves with a handy source of food during their transient stay on the nursery meadow.

Then, during late afternoon of a day little different from the ones which had preceded it, a restlessness became apparent among the members of the pack. The leader had made several short trips away from the meadow during the day, and upon his last return, the others gathered around him, their tails wagging in expectation. The gray bitch seemed impatient with the four pups as they attempted to draw her into play, and she ignored their advances. Then, whining low in her throat, she issued a signal to the litter, one which the pups had never before been asked to obey, before moving off to leave them obediently sitting in the high grass. Swinging along in the wake of the black male, she stopped to look back only once before vanishing, with the others, into the spruce.

CHAPTER 7

There were two moose on the small clearing that lay less than a hundred yards from the shallow and meandering Wood River. The nine-hundred-pound cow and her calf of the year had spent most of August's shortening days close to the place, and the broad gravel and silt bars along the adjacent half mile of the silty river were cut liberally with the tracks, both old and new, left by their splayed hooves.

The three-hundred-pound calf, a bull, was one of a pair the cow had dropped in late May, less than a mile from the small clearing along the river. That there had been twins was, in itself, somewhat unusual, given the scarcity of winter browse the cow's range in this part of the sprawling flats still offered.

Moose, the largest cloven-hoofed animal remaining upon the North American Continent, are browsers, and subsist upon woody branches and twigs throughout most of the long Arctic winter. Their long, yellow-stained incisor teeth are ideally suited for pruning the fibrous branches of the willow and aspen, which comprise almost the entirety of their diet during the seven months of cold. The cow will require almost forty pounds of such cuttings to sustain her on a daily basis.

The dense stands of willow brush growing along and

upon each braided river bar had long before been cropped back to a height of four feet or less by feeding moose, a point at which the willows' annual growth no longer was adequate for the needs of the cow and others of her kind that wintered there. As a result, she had spent five of the six years since her birth existing upon a substandard diet.

During the winter following the birth of her first calf, a lack of food within the youngster's reach, and a massive layer of snow, had caused its slow death by starvation. This had occurred during the cow's third year, and though she had remained healthy, the skimpy winter diets had, until this year, robbed her of the capacity to bear the twin calves, which, during times of plenty, are normal.

The cow and her calf had bedded among the clumps of brittle six-foot-high grass and sedges that bordered the small clearing and walled off its margin where it gave way to dense spruce and birch farther from the river. A cool wind had gusted persistently throughout the day, making the shelter afforded by the nodding grass a welcome thing to the big animals as they lay contentedly chewing cuds and dozing in the meager warmth of a pale sun.

Body size is seemingly equatable with security among wild creatures that compete in a world of predators, one of the factors that has enabled the moose to survive the relentless process of evolutionary selection. Such security often exacts a terrible compensation, however, as it had during the fourth day after the cow's most recent calving.

The black bear—a three-year-old boar—had followed the winter-gaunt cow throughout each of the several days that preceded the onset of her labor. She had almost grown accustomed to his constant presence, and the boar, in turn, had shown what appeared to be only a casual interest in her. Then the shuffling bear had vanished as suddenly as he had appeared during the night she felt the first gut cramps of the impending birth.

The cow had seen many bears during her life, for they were plentiful along the Wood River, and this one's presence failed to pique even the mild curiosity she had felt as a younger animal. Through simple chance, however, she had never encountered a bear during the terminus of a pregnancy, though conscious realization of this fact was, of course, beyond the scope of her intelligence.

The black bear was a small one, weighing less than 150 pounds. He had left the place where he had slept during the past winter almost two weeks before he happened onto the cow. The boar had stayed beneath the tangle of spruce roots and blowdowns longer than was customary before being rudely awakened during mid-April by an avalanche of slushy snow. Reluctantly emerging into the cold sunshine of spring, he had traveled lethargically and erratically along the low winter-dead ridges near the river, grazing upon horsetail fern and eventually the tender catkins of willow.

Standing among the bog tufts of an old burn, the cow had licked her two calves dry, then watched the roan twins stand less than an hour later. Both appeared healthy, and were soon butting her for the supply of milk that survival required.

The passage of those first few days had been enough time for the fiercely protective instinctive urges possessed by the cow to mature, and when the bear reappeared she bristled, silently signaling her knob-kneed calves to stand close against her brisket.

The bear continued to bide his time, once more seemingly disinterested in the presence of the cow, and his tactics eventually had their desired effect. Familiarity with the presence of the bear coupled with a typically short attention span caused the cow to grow tired of staring at the intruder that dozed on the moundlike muskrat lodge nearby. It was this momentary carelessness that caused her to make a mistake. Swinging her massive head, she turned away from the boar, and with her calves in tow started to move away.

The bear's attack was in sharp contrast to his slow-moving presence during past days, and his silent sidestepping charge was betrayed only by the tearing sounds his claws made as they dug greedily at the punky soil and matted vegetation of the burn. Fleeting seconds and the blurred advance of the bear left the trailing calf torn and bleating pitifully as it dragged its crippled hindquarters, struggling to once more gain security beneath the cow's belly. Even as the cow turned in the sucking bog mud she had entered, the bear retreated to the dubious safety of the muskrat lodge, where he shook his glossy coat and proceeded to lick his sticky forepaws.

The calf died within the hour that followed, but the cow stood nearby long after a cold dusk settled over the marshy burn. Then she slowly moved off, her remaining calf crowded close between her forelegs. For the bear, the meal that followed was adequate, and enough of the fifteen-pound calf remained to warrant covering it with his body as he slept soundly through the hours of midday.

By the following evening, both calf and bear were absent from the burn, and only a few scattered reddish hairs floated in the shallow stagnant water that was already refreezing in the returning cold of the spring night.

A white-rumped marsh hawk swooped soundlessly overhead, its shadow lingering momentarily on the undulating sea of dead grass that concealed the resting moose. The harrier and his mate had nested in the sedges of a dry slough nearby, and two immature birds had accompanied the adults during past weeks as they hunted ceaselessly for mice among the swampy places which bordered the river.

The cow and her calf paid no more attention to the hawks than they did to the ravens that often gathered to croak and chirp as they hovered over the daytime beds of the moose. Except during periods of rain, the arrival of the birds had been a daily event during the summer, and they had become as much a part of the cow's life as the grass in which she slept. They had, in other years, watched the birth of her calves and her consumption of the bluish afterbirth, and one day would likely share her own remains with foxes and others that subsisted in such a way.

The cow's inability to cough up a final ball of partially chewed grass and the hollow rumblings of her partitioned stomach signaled the end of another day far more eloquently than the cooling air that followed the retreating sun. Grunting deeply as she gained her feet in the deep grass, she deposited a dark, shapeless pile of dung in the pressed oval where she had slept. Later, with a winter diet of woody stems, even this would change, her droppings assuming the coffee-bean shape of winter. Finally, after standing motionless for several minutes, she moved slowly out onto the small clearing, and her calf followed.

It was still far too early in the year for the cow to feel the hormone-induced need called the rut, or breeding season. Almost another full month would pass before the arrival of that period of several weeks during which she would enter the two or three days of estrus and seek actively for the attentions of a bull.

During the previous autumn, in early October, she had once more shared the single-minded attentions of a huge bull with a temporary following of nearly a dozen other cows, called a pod. An eight-year-old, bearing antlers that spanned sixty-five inches, he had mounted her eagerly on numerous occasions. Well into his prime, he had already lost some of the fat which had brought his weight during early autumn down to just more than thirteen hundred pounds, the result of a loss of appetite for anything that did not resemble a sexual encounter.

In company with the big bull during the autumn past had been a three-year-old of the same sex. The youngster boasted only smallish, shovel-sized antlers, yet stood almost seven feet at his shoulder hump. Though nearly matching the herd bull in height, the youngster was content in his abstinence where the cows were concerned, a factor which undoubtedly caused the larger bull to tolerate his presence.

Like the others that joined and then left the bull's breeding group, the cow had watched as he punctured the ribs of several would-be contenders and sent them packing. His sheer body size and antler width facilitated the bulls' dispatch without adding to the well-healed splits in his own ears and the puckered scars in his velvety nose.

This year, when the approaching rut became reality, the cow would once again grunt her high-pitched moaning call during the frost-rimed evenings as she moved among the low hog's-back ridges and swales that backed the river. With the onset of the coming rut, she would not move far from her summer pasture, nor would she travel in a sustained manner. With the weather growing colder, she would, however, spend less time bedded during the daylight hours, remaining on the riverbars long after the sun had burned the dense ground fog from the water. Finally, and as had happened during all of the late autumns of her life, her quest would be rewarded by the deep, rasping grunts of a bull.

Her calf would remain with her as she became a temporary part of the bull's coterie of cows, and in her turn she would be mounted several times when her estrus catalyzed the physical act of copulation. Because the huge bull would be virile and the process efficient, conception would be almost guaranteed, but, if by some quirk she did not become pregnant, another period of estrus would occur a month after the first. The process of seeking another bull would then have to be repeated, but her chances of being bred would be decreased. Even if she became pregnant as a result of a late breeding, the chances for survival of the calf she would drop late in the summer of the next year would be greatly lessened because of its immaturity at winter's onset.

A gestation of two hundred and forty-five days had been required to make fifteen-pound moose calves of the microscopic cell clusters which resulted from last year's rut. The normal efficiency of the process which would soon be repeated had already been halved by the loss of one of her twins, though her recollection of the event had dimmed and vanished brief hours after its occurrence. A sedentary creature of simple but precise habit, the cow lived a life of a long series of interconnected but unremembered events, which through repetition resulted in learning. Even her returns each evening to the open expanses found along the river were the result of habit formed during many summers. Seclusion with her newborn calf demanded that she remain in the dense willows and high grass of the insect-saturated bog holes during the hot, windless days of July and August. Only with the cooling of each evening did she escape from the torment of mosquitoes, gnats, and spotted deer flies by regularly visiting the river.

The calf followed the cow as she moved slowly toward the murmuring river, their hooves sucking in the gelatinous mud, leaving deep-gouted tracks which quickly filled with brackish water saturated with foul-smelling methane gas. Though early frost had quickly reduced the clouds of insects and cooler weather had rendered the survivors less active, habit was difficult to change even were there a reason to do so, and she would once again fill her belly with the cold silty water before spending the coming night feeding.

Cow and calf reached the fringe of willow and alder that still separated them from the river and paused to eat a few mouthfuls of wrinkled, dark-green alder leaves before disappearing from sight. Tendrils of fog were already forming over the river, making its roiled surface resemble molten lead as the evening's chill mixed with the warmer layer of air that lingered there.

Reappearing on the broad, driftwood-littered gravel bar a short time later, the animals paused one last time to feed briefly among the willows that defined its margin, then leisurely moved on toward the river. Bankside spruces were already silhouetted against the western sky, and a pair of golden-eyed ducks swung low overhead, their wings whistling as they dodged the river's sharp bends while moving upstream toward some unknown resting place.

The wind that had gusted during the day had died, and the silence was broken only by the crunching of hooves in the loose gravel as the two animals moved haltingly toward the water. There was no reason to hurry, and they stopped often, the cow testing the content of the cooling air that washed gently from a downriver direction. Then, turning her head, she flicked her mulelike ears and belched quietly, the pendulous bell of loose skin at her throat swaying gently.

The heavy, damp air told her nothing more than it had on most of the uncounted evenings she had engaged in this ritual of returning to the river. Only the faint lingering tang of spruce pitch, the mild slatelike odor of the water itself, and the incense of swamp mud and decaying leaves were present. Then, with her calf going ahead, the cow crossed the belt of sand left by the receding water.

Shoulder to shoulder, they moved into the river, splashing quietly in the shallow opaque water that quickly became belly-deep. Then the cow lowered her massive head and sucked noisily. Somewhere behind the two animals a horned owl talked resonantly in the deepening twilight, to be answered by the softer call of another in the spruce-shrouded distance.

Coughing deeply, the cow blew a spray of fine vapor from her pendulous muzzle, and it condensed cloudlike on the chill air as she resumed her drinking. The sound caused the leader of the St. George Creek pack to twitch involuntarily and lower his head, flattening himself on the sandy cutbank from which he had watched the moose for some time. Less than two hundred yards separated moose and wolf, and the small movement made by his buff-colored son who lay nearby as he licked sand from a cut on the big pad of his forepaw was undetectable in the gathering darkness.

❧ CHAPTER 8

The long afternoon hours had passed slowly for the gray bitch's pups during their first day alone on the nursery meadow. At first, the newness of still-unexplored tunnels beneath the wind-tossed grass had held their attention, but this soon gave way to a vacant loneliness.

They ventured repeatedly to the edge of the meadow to be close to the dwindling scent left by the departing pack, but always dutifully returned to the shelter and darkness of tall grass where the old bitch had left them. Here their loneliness, rather than the chill wind that hissed among the tall ocher-colored tops of the dense marsh grass and flattened them with its passage, made them shiver and shift their positions repeatedly. Then, as afternoon shadows lengthened, they whimpered among themselves, and their collective crying spoke eloquently of the misery produced by the absence of their elders.

The pack had traveled in a northeasterly direction after leaving the nursery meadow, a course which carried them farther out onto the flats, and though the black wolf set a slow pace, by evening more than fifteen miles separated the pack from the gray bitch's litter.

By habit, the wolves followed the path of least resistance as they moved across the land. Deep-cut moose trails became more numerous and offered easy, though indirect, passage where they snaked among the stunted spruce that stood in profusion on low ridges. Nameless dry creekbeds lay dished and devoid of water, their shrunken surfaces checkered with their drying, and these too provided avenues of unhampered travel along which the pack trotted easily, leaving a common line of splayed tracks in the dusty silt.

The air on the flats was alive with the smells of autumn, and the wolves moved through aspen and birch groves whose leaves had already been touched by light frost. Cold nights and the shortening days had turned many to gold and they shimmered against the pale-blue sky like pond water beneath a gusting wind. Red viburnum, or wild cranberry, spread heavy musk from branches burdened with clusters of translucent red fruit. Scattered everywhere in the shadows of larch and spruce, and in the wetness of boggy places, were plump blueberries, the dusty whiteness of their puckered skins attesting to their ripeness and the early frost.

In the gathering dusk, the wolves had flushed small flocks of ruffed grouse and clucking slate-colored spruce hens, the birds settling in nearby trees only to flutter back to their feeding on clusters of waxy twinberry and wild mushrooms with the wolves' passage.

The flats were composed of almost continuous marshland, and the pack listened to the clucks and clicking of feeding waterfowl as it moved steadily. The reedy quacking of mallards mixed with the piping calls of widgeon and carried clearly from the safety of open water.

The clamor of the pups died as the soft darkness descended over the meadow. They were, as always, hungry, but loneliness accentuated by the damp chill of the approaching night left them with little desire to chase voles and shrews in the long grass. Unlike foxes of the same age, the pups still knew nothing of the actual process of killing, for they had not accompanied the adults on a hunt.

Wolves, perhaps because of their great intelligence and a life-style based upon the concept of the pack with its complex behavioral demands, must learn the process of hunting and the act of killing to make it a successful venture, in which survival is the reward. Instinctive hunting behavior, the ability to function that is present before birth, seems subdued among wolves. Though pursuit of moving objects is based upon instinct, and from this simple activity stems the sophistication of co-operative hunting as pups become adults, even the act of killing an immobile prey animal must be learned by wolves through practice, repeated observation, and individual experimentation.

Unlike wolves, fox kits are whelped with an unerring ability to not only catch their food but to kill it with a quick bite at the base of the neck. Wolves bring with them only the potential to learn as they start life, and, perhaps incongruously, it is this characteristic which reveals their greater intelligence when compared to the smaller canines. The potential to learn did not benefit the gray bitch's pups, however, as they fidgeted in the grass of the nursery meadow, and with the passage of each slow hour, their hunger grew to belly-cramping proportions.

Even the sounds of the night were different here. The pups had never listened to the muted conversations of owls, for there were none among the treeless slopes that held the den meadow. They listened also to the squeaks of dead trees as they rubbed together in the vagrant breeze that rose and fell. Then a different sound reached their ears, and the largest male rose slowly and took a few tentative steps toward the rasping clicks that emanated from the depths of the spruce shadows nearby. Moonlight dappled his narrow, dun-colored back as, wagging his tail, he moved toward the source of his curiosity.

The porcupine had spent the day sleeping soundly in a small spruce not far from the edge of the nursery meadow.

The tree was one of several in the area that he used for his all-day naps. Its selection, like the others, had apparently been the result of simple random choice, possibly encouraged by the tree's brush-free base, trunk size, and the underbark it once offered. The bark had long ago been gnawed from the spruce, leaving its trunk and lower branches bare, and, as a result, the tree was dead. Old piles of the porky's wormlike droppings attested to its one-time worth as a food source as well as the frequency with which he used the place as a roost.

Like the ancestors of the St. George Creek pack, the quill pig's forebears first appeared on the portion of the globe destined to be called Alaska almost thirty million years before. Also like the wolves, he had changed little in appearance during the passage of the millenia. Both the most recent form taken by the changing land and the evolutionary process had been kind to the porcupine, the former providing the quiet isolation in a world of bark he preferred, and the latter a supply of hollow, barb-tipped quills which covered his upper body and provided almost perfectly for his protection from grizzly bears and wolf pups.

The porky, a thirty-pound boar, had already waited longer than usual to awaken and hitch his way down the wear-smoothed spruce trunk. Darkness was almost complete as he paused by habit at the tree's base to lick his front paws, while grunting softly to himself as he prepared for his nocturnal wanderings. Then, content in a solidarity of purpose which included little beyond the procurement of another sustaining meal of bark, and still whistling and grunting deeply, he moved off among the clubfoot moss beneath the dark trees.

His slow, rolling gait took him only a short distance before he stopped at the base of a small birch sapling. Then, supporting himself on his thick muscular tail, he began to gnaw slowly at the tender bark with his large, rodent's incisors. Like the beaver, he too discarded the rough and woody outer bark, seeking only the whitish cambium layer, with its slippery, starchy flavor. Finally, after an hour, and once again mewing contentedly, he moved on.

It was much later when the porky returned by a circuitous path to the single antler palm that lay partially embedded in the damp moss beneath the spruces. Though his nose wrinkled ceaselessly as he waddled among the shadows, he found the antler more by chance than as a result of scenting it. The palm, a small one, had been dropped during some January past by a bull moose, to be replaced the following spring by a new and larger set.

The rasping of powerful teeth on the porous calcium and phosphorus-rich antler carried well on the cold stillness of the night air, and the dun pup encountered little difficulty finding the source of the sound. Wagging his tail slowly, he circled the porcupine, then sat on his haunches to watch the curious animal that paid little attention to his presence.

It was, perhaps, the quill pig's apparent lack of interest that caused the big pup's curiosity to grow with each passing minute. Whining and panting, he once more began to circle the porky. Then, after barking several times, he moved away and returned to the others in the deep grass of the meadow. Several hours later, the dun pup heard the rasping sounds which attended the porky's return to the antler, and without hesitation he once more followed his ears to the source of his curiosity. This time, the rest of the litter followed.

Made bold by his earlier encounter with the porky, the big pup assumed the initiative by moving dangerously close and stretching his muzzle toward the big rodent. Then instinctive caution caused him to move back quickly as the gnawing ceased. Had the porcupine been fleet of foot, or even inclined to run, the pups would, most likely, have relinquished their apparent advantage. As it was, however, the stodgy quill pig possessed neither ability, and the resumed grating of his teeth coupled with the presence of the other pups provided the dun male with the courage required to reach for the porky with his front paw.

Somehow sensing the nearness of the pup's foot, the porcupine drew himself into a tight ball, tucking his short, quill-laced tail under him. Then the light touch of the young wolf's paw caused him to stiffen and arch his back just enough to embed a single quill in the tender space between the wolf's toes. The dun pup jerked backward, sat down, and began licking his foot.

The mild pain caused by the solitary quill should have been a warning, but instead it merely added to his building frustration. Though superficially embedded, the quill remained stuck in the soft skin of the pup's foot, and his attempts to remove it by licking only produced more pain as the barbs worked deeper. Then, ignoring his paw, the dun pup barked shrilly at the porky, who had once more resumed his stoic gnawing on the antler. The rest of the pups moved back, confused by the dun male's excitement, and watched from several feet away. The porcupine moved away from the antler, turning slowly and reaching with his blunt nose as he sought an obvious avenue of escape from the confusion of the tiny clearing.

As the porky moved, so did the dun pup. Leaping forward, he closed his mouth deeply on the deceptive furry softness of the quill pig's back. The porcupine, which until now had appeared sluggish and almost unaware of the pup's presence, once more arched its body and, in the same instant, whipped its muscular tail sideways. The pup's attack and the porky's retaliation came in a blur of motion, too fast for the other pups to watch.

Searing pain caused the pup to recoil backward and somersault into the spruce shadows. The explosion in his mouth made him scream as he rolled in the moss, clawing at his head and muzzle in a panic of effort to rid himself of the more than a dozen quills that were now deeply embedded in his tongue, throat, and lips. Initial panic and surprise rapidly gave way to confused flight as he ran blindly among the shadow-dappled spaces between the dark spruces. His continued wailing frightened the rest of the pups, and for lack of a better place to go, they retreated to the familiarity of the meadow.

An hour passed before the big pup returned to the place of encounter with the quill pig. Whining pitifully, and nearly exhausted from his efforts to rid himself of the pain that caused blood to seep from his mouth and stain his chest, he skirted the abandoned antler on his way to the dubious security of the nursery meadow. The porcupine had ambled away after waiting for a brief period, and the false light of the foggy dawn found him contemplating the long, slow climb back to the fork in the spruce where he would once more sleep peacefully through the coming day.

It had been early evening as the St. George Creek pack reached the Wood River Buttes, where they moved single file across the steep slope above the river. The buttes, an isolated and short chain of hills, were a prominent feature on the flats, visible for many miles in all directions. Their bases were liberally carpeted with short spruce, which gave way higher up to dense stands of small aspen and birch. Their tops were bald, devoid of any growth other than ground plants, moss, sedges, and wild rose. These were special places for the black leader, and he brought the pack here often during the autumn. Because of his familiarity, the big male swung higher still along the steep slope, angling upward toward the nearest dome. As the pack emerged on the open ground, the black went directly but cautiously to a single dead birch which stood in the clearing.

The tree had been stripped of its white bark to a point almost seven feet above its gnarled base during some past autumn by a bull moose as he patiently rubbed his antlers to rid them of the soft chestnut-colored skin called velvet. The furlike covering had served its purpose of temporarily protecting the new antlers while they passed from soft and tender to bony hardness. Then, with maturity, the bull had spent many hours scraping them on the little birch.

The cleaning of his antlers was synonymous with the onset of the rut, and because of the amount of time he spent in the clearing, he had dug shallow depressions in the dusty soil, urinated into them, and then rolled his massive body in the wet earth. The ritual excited him and with the passage of a week he had almost completely lost his appetite for food; and the coming mating season became a consummate obsession. His rolling left his powerful shoulders, brisket, and hips rank with the cloying musk that bespoke his readiness to breed.

It had been the urine-heavy scent of the bull that had brought the black male to the place initially. Snow had already fallen, and the moose had moved to the meadows near the base of the buttes, thus making himself more available to the cows that his scent would surely attract, but his musk remained strong in the depressions he had dug. The pack leader and his followers had also rolled in the scent of the bull, but only because of its intoxicating potency rather than any sex-related stimulation on their part. Following his discovery of the place, the big male had then returned frequently, his visits finally motivated by habit after the disappearance of the bull's scent.

Other packs had also visited here during past times, for the place was at the recognized edge of the black wolf's domain. Because of this, it bore more importance to all concerned than did similar places located well within the range of the St. George Creek pack. It was also a place to be approached with caution by the big black and the others.

Though through simple coincidence the black had never encountered other wolves on the open crowns of the buttes, such a meeting would have dire consequences were it to occur. It was a no-man's land, a place of dubious ownership, and one to be fought over in a dispute for inclusion in the territory of each pack.

Familiarity with the place caused the big male to raise his hind leg and spurt his own urine on the tree's red under-bark. Circling, he then pawed the ground beneath the tree, and finally squatted and once more partially emptied his bladder. The gray bitch immediately did likewise, her urine overlapping that of her mate's. The rest of the pack members urinated in turn nearby, then dug vigorously with their hind feet to scatter the scent. In minutes, the area near the small birch had become saturated with the odor of the pack, and would remain so for many months, especially with periodic additions to its potency. It would serve as an olfactory reminder of the pack's passage and its pre-emption of the buttes as part of its territory. The presence of the scent place and its meaning would be respected by other wolves that would pass by.

There were other signs of the pack's visits to the open ground near the birch. Piles of old droppings, many bleached white and consisting almost entirely of packed moose hair, were scattered in the dry moss and the still evident depressions left by the moose. These were winter scats, and they too helped form the marker along the northerly boundary of the St. George Creek pack's range. As if to assure their continued presence, the gray bitch squatted and defecated scantily before stretching her body and shaking to rid her pelt of the acid dust she had rolled in.

Later, after idling at the scent place for almost an hour, the black leader had chewed briefly on the scarred trunk of the birch, urinated one last time, then trotted purposefully downslope toward the river. The soft sounds of the flowing water became clearly audible as he swung parallel to the river, moving once more in a downstream direction. As the pack reached level, swampy ground, moose trails again became plentiful beneath the dense stands of spruces, making travel easier. Then, moving single file, the wolves trotted in almost complete darkness beneath the dense clones of alder that choked the river bottom.

Once clear of the buttes, which had become mere outlines in the dusk, the black wolf picked up the pace. Dense underbrush gave way to open gravel bars as he led the pack closer to the river itself. By habit, they would now hug the watercourse, utilizing the open sand and gravel that made the bars along the inside of each turn in the river. Each convolution that produced such openings also made an undercut bank where the flow turned back on itself. Here, with few exceptions, the dropping water level had left shelf-like ledges, and the pack used them in its passage. In such places the individual tracks of each wolf became indistinguishable as twelve pairs of splayed feet moved along a common trail. The leader was also adept at slipping beneath slumped trees, or sweepers, collapsed by the river's flow, and he traveled without pause.

Once, rounding a sharp bend in the river, the pack surprised a single moose standing in the current at midstream. The barren cow paused only long enough to identify the floating shadows before splashing noisily to the opposite bank, which she climbed easily before disappearing among the permafrost-stunted spruce of a swampy opening above the river. The pack had not followed.

Later still, and in semidarkness, the river's surface appeared silver where the current roiled and washed over gravel shallows. In the rapidly cooling air, streamers of fog formed over the water as the pack stopped to investigate the measly remains of several salmon that had drifted into the shallows after their death. The receding water had stranded the bodies of the fish, and the white moss of decay had already softened them, making their putrid odor easy to follow.

Though the Wood River was not known as a place where heavy migration of king and chum salmon occurred during the autumn spawning movement, there were always enough of the oily fish to make the gravel bars attractive to lynx, foxes, ravens, and wolves. After laying eggs in the upper, clearer reaches of the river, the fish died as a normal postscript to their lives in salt water. Their blind travels required the entirety of each summer. From the Bering Sea, they followed the Yukon and Tanana upstream, finally swinging into the inconspicuous shallows of the Wood's mouth. The run would continue until the river was partially frozen, the red- and green-striped chums being the last travelers to arrive.

The pack paused on the silt bar where the rotting fish lay, the black and his sons immediately rolling in several of the carcasses, which bore little resemblance to their original form. No wolf was able to resist, and as the pack continued under the paleness of the climbing moon, its members bore a stench of tangible proportions, and it was this scent that had reached the flaring nostrils of the big cow moose as she stood drinking with her calf. The discovery caused her to abruptly raise her massive head, the water of her drinking dribbling back into the river from her pendulous snout.

Though in the shifting breeze the scent of rotten fish masked the odor of wolf, several minutes had passed slowly before the heavy scent carried on the almost still air. Unable to detect the direction from which it came, the cow stamped her front hoof, driving it deeply into the soft riverbed. Then, blowing once, she retraced her steps to the gravel bar she had used when coming to the river, her calf shouldering close.

River water ran from their bellies as they paused, the cow

once more reaching for more of the scent that had driven her from the stream. Here it was still present though less powerful, and it caused her to lay her ears back among the now erect roach hairs of her upper neck. The same uncertainty which had caused her to pause then motivated her to move, and with the calf ahead of her, she trotted slowly across the broad gravel bar, moving in an upriver direction.

The black leader and his son were up and moving with the cow's first step, and they swung quickly along the deep-gouted tracks that led toward the bar's end where the moose had quickly disappeared into the dense willow and alder. The wolves did not need the visual clue provided by the tracks in the pale moonlight, for the cow's scent lay heavy on the quiet air.

The moose moved several hundred yards along the river before stopping once more on yet another of its broad gravel bars, the cow's big hooves sinking in the silt of a sandy depression dug by the current during high water. Then, breathing heavily with the sudden exertion of movement and the mild fear generated by the heavy scents of rotten fish and wolves, she nosed the calf at her side, and the smaller animal moved closer to her heaving belly. Only muted gurglings and the occasional slap of a collapsing silt bank somewhere upriver broke the silence.

The gray bitch, her adult son, and the white resident females heard the movement of the cow and calf as they left the water and fled along the riverbar. They too followed along, hidden by the deep shadow beneath the bankside spruces, until they joined the black and the other buff wolf just as they entered the dense alder at the bar's end.

The pack flowed as a series of shadows, strung out and silent, onto the gravel spit where the cow had stopped. The moose saw them immediately, and once again her hackles rose and she lowered her head and turned to meet the wolves. Sheer momentum carried the black leader's son to within a few feet of her, and he skidded as he stopped short of an actual collision.

Wagging his plumed tail, the black trotted boldly to the buff wolf's side, his long tongue lolling as he panted with the mild exertion of the brief chase. Then he sat upright, watching the cow from a distance of only a few yards. The rest of the pack members spread out along the rear of the bar upon which the moose stood, seemingly content to continue to idle as they had since the black male had watched the moose from the first discovery.

The buff began licking the small cut on his forefoot, and given the silence which hung over the riverbar, the scene took on an almost unnatural quality. Though an atmosphere of armed truce prevailed, it was not apparent in the actions of either wolves or moose. Instead, the almost casual appearance of the cow and the confused obedience of her calf, who now crowded close to her chest and forelegs, lent an almost macabre touch to the scenario. The impression was heightened by the slow wagging of the gray bitch's tail as she walked slowly into the willow stubs along the bar's rear edge.

One of the owls talked briefly, its call distance-muffled now, as the cow shifted her position slightly. She watched the movement of the buff at the leader's side as he rose and shook sand from his coat before lying down once more. The black whine-yawned as he too settled to his belly on the cool silt, his attention drawn to the sounds made by his second grown son as he attempted to draw the gray bitch into a romp among the dew-drenched willows nearby.

More than an hour passed with little change in the position of the participants. The cow had gradually circled where she stood, placing the calf between herself and the river, and the silt immediately beneath her was deeply cut with her tracks. The black wolf, apparently becoming bored with his vigil near the head-hung cow, had moved slowly into the willows and had been replaced by the other buff.

The sky to the northeast once more silhouetted the spruce beyond the river against pale lemon light as the black returned to the river. Followed by his mate, he strode aggressively toward the cow, causing her once more to raise her mane and lower her big ears. Circling the moose, the big wolf diverted her attention momentarily, and she turned slowly to keep him in sight. The gray bitch now moved quickly toward the moose's exposed flank, but stopped short in a shower of wet sand as the cow flicked her hind foot.

The old bitch retreated, and was followed immediately by her mate. She moved to the far end of the silt bar, where she lapped briefly but noisily at the cold water. Then, as if by some silent agreement, both wolves trotted away in an upriver direction. The two dun males followed, but only after staging a final mock charge at the cow and calf. The two resident females swung out of the willows well away from the moose to rejoin the moving pack, which disappeared silently beneath the shadowed undercut bank beyond.

It is possible but not likely that some vague recollection of the loss of her other calf caused the cow to stand her ground on the silt bar until well after the sun filtered through the river fog.

With the coming of the new day, Canada jays swooped over the water, their calls echoless in the still air as they searched for a meal, and the croaking of a single raven was heard as the bird approached from some unknown roost to the west. Finally, cow and calf left the river, moving purposefully into the dense willow in search of a place where they would once more spend the day bedded in the deep grass of the marsh. By then the St. George Creek pack was well on its way toward the far-off nursery meadow, their coats drenched with heavy morning dew.

❦ CHAPTER 9

The hollow ivory and black quills, each tipped with minute, hook-shaped barbs, were deeply embedded in the dun pup's mouth and throat. Others, the shorter stiffer quills from the porcupine's tail, protruded dartlike from his narrow chest and upper forelegs.

Instinctive habit had caused the quill pig to face away from danger, and as a result the young wolf's leap, triggered by excited curiosity rather than any conscious desire to kill, had come from the worst possible direction. Simple inertia had driven the porcupine's longer back quills into the pup's mouth. Then, even as the initial shock of searing pain stopped the pup's jaws from actually closing upon the porcupine's body, the big rodent's tail had switched once, driving many of the dark-colored, stubby quills that sheathed it into the pup's chest and legs.

Dazed and suffocating in a confusion of pain, the pup ran blindly for several minutes before finally stopping to paw at his head and lick his upper legs. This merely produced more pain, and he soon found that he could not close his mouth because of the quills that it contained. With free-flowing, blood-streaked saliva staining the hair of his throat and chest, and once more wailing shrilly, the pup panicked and rolled wildly in the darkness of wet grass and wild-rose thorns.

The other pups had retreated immediately to the long grass of the meadow, where they were joined later by the stricken male. Still whimpering pitifully, he crowded close to the small female, the blood that now seeped steadily from his muzzle staining her shoulders. Like the others, she backed away, confused and frightened by the undefined actions of her brother and the scent of his blood.

The hapless pup spent the rest of the interminable night in abject misery. Each small movement brought added pain and caused the quills to work deeper into his body, where the barbs held them fast as they gained new purchase. Much later, as the first light of dawn filtered through the dense layer of fog that blanketed the meadow, he shivered violently in the cold dampness.

Why the black leader and the rest of the pack had not pressed an attack upon the moose calf on the river is not easily explained. Perhaps the big male and his mate had somehow sensed the advantage of position held by the cow on the unobstructed silt bar where she had chosen to make her stand. Both wolves had, on many occasions, faced the swiftness of big hooves, and each bore the node-like thickenings of scar tissue on ribs that had been broken during such encounters.

After leaving the river, the pack had traveled with more purpose than had attended their movements of the day before. The good weather of past weeks continued, though the flats once more whispered under chill wind gusts from the west, gusts that had begun shortly after daybreak. The heavy fog layer that whitened the flats had moved rapidly ahead of the rising wind, thickening in dimension as it rose in the warming air before dissipating. Until then, the sun had remained invisible to the wolves as they moved in a shadowless gloom of dripping brush and down timber.

Even the usually vociferous Canada jays and red squirrels were absent as the pack moved steadily cross-country toward the far-off nursery meadow. The black led his followers in a southeasterly direction which, at first, paralleled the Wood and then swung away from its course. The two buffs left the rest on several occasions, unable to resist the temptation of chasing the long-legged snowshoe hares that announced their presence by thumping the punky ground with their oversized hind feet. Such warning signals to others of their kind were well known to the wolves, but no advantage was gained and their efforts went virtually unrewarded. Only one hare was caught by the gray bitch as, flushed by one of her sons, it ghosted across her path.

Like the graceful short-tailed weasel and the ptarmigan, the hares were already showing the change from summer brown to winter white, and their ears, heads, and feet contrasted sharply with the shadowed darkness as they loped silently through the tunnels of grass their runways made.

The mysterious transition in body color involved an actual change in hair color rather than the shedding of one coat and its replacement with another, the process seemingly catalyzed by shortening periods of daylight as the autumn deepened. The change would not be complete until snow already lay upon the flats, and the interim period would once more make the animals stand out almost luminously, to be easily seen by owls, hawks, foxes, wolves, and a host of others that preyed upon them. With the new snow, however, they would blend perfectly with the whiteness, only their large eyes and tracks betraying their position among the willow clumps and dark spruces.

Though the wolves would catch many of the hares during the months ahead, such hunting would involve exercise that burned as much energy as the few pounds of edible meat would provide. Of the big predators that lived on the broad flats, only the slab-sided lynx was capable of utilizing the snowshoe hares as a reliable source of staple food. Masters of the brief, blurred attack, the tan-mottled bobtailed cats were numerous only when the hare population was heavy.

During late morning, the pack reached a trickle of tannin-dark water called Fish Creek. They paused here just as the sun broke through the thinning layer of ground fog, its fingerlike rays gradually warming the sodden earth. Tendrils of steam rose, regenerating the process of fog production among the dripping yellow leaves, a process which would end with the drying of the flats themselves. Only then would the frost that rimed the layers of fallen leaves where they collected at the margins of shaded ponds melt once more.

As the air warmed, the black wolf increased his pace and the pack followed single file. The wolves traveled in the familiar trotting gait which coupled distance-eating speed with physical ease and resulted in a curiously efficient floating movement. With heads down and tails drooped, the six animals effortlessly moved through the complex network of trails and countless openings, fanning out only when brush and down timber made it necessary.

On a few occasions they stopped long enough to urinate and refresh the potency of scent posts along the route. Such places varied from the bases of saplings to bog tufts and sometimes patches of bare ground. Most of these posts were places that the wolves had used during past times, others were new to them. Then, at a particularly well-used place along the margin of a dry pond, the pack paused as a unit, the gray bitch and one of the resident females defecating loosely among the dense bog tufts.

Both animals suffered the inroads of common intestinal roundworms, and their thin stools were diffused with the eggs of the parasites. In actuality, all members of the pack supported infestations of the worms in varying degrees, and had done so since before birth. Even had they not contracted the migrating larvae of these parasites while still encased in their dams' reproductive tracts, each would have ingested eggs that existed in viable form on the moss and in the ground near the den. Such eggs are microscopic, and remain present long after the fecal material in which they were carried washes away.

For wolves, the roundworm cycle is unavoidable, and the animals become unknowing hosts for the parasite. If the wolf is in good health and has adequate food, the worms produce few obvious ill effects except, perhaps, for the mild cramps that the gray bitch would have counted among her other age-induced frailties.

After leaving the dry pond, and still following the course of Fish Creek, the pack began the long, almost imperceptible ascent into the low hills and shallow gullies that preceded the Alaska Range. Arriving there during midafternoon, the black swung away from the creek, and the pack began to traverse a looping dogleg which carried to the west. The new course would take the wolves directly to the nursery meadow.

The gray bitch heard the thin whining of her pups before she reached them, and nudged the shoulder of one of her adult sons as he trotted next to her. Something in the sound caused her to quicken her pace, while wagging her tail uncertainly.

The porcupine had, as was his preference, spent the day high among the branches of the dead spruce. In his dull manner, he had quickly forgotten the wolf pups that his ears told him were still nearby, their periodic whining having served only to rouse him briefly from lethargic sleep. His belly bulged with yellow-spruce bark that would produce more of the puffy fat that already layered his rotund body and formed a lacy net among his intestines. Secure from all enemies, he mewed softly in his sleep, tucked his short tail closer to the trunk of the spruce, and was unaware of the pack as it passed almost directly beneath the roost tree.

Long, slanting shadows of the range enveloped the nursery meadow as the gray bitch met her gyrating pups in the short trees that bordered it. Hoisting their hind quarters off the ground with her nose, she sensed the absence of the biggest pup, and ignoring their muzzle-grasping impatience, she trotted quickly to the place among the clumps of long grass where their scent lay heaviest. It was here that she discovered the dun-colored male.

Though his chest was still streaked with dried saliva and brownish bloodstains, the pup had recovered from the initial shock of his encounter with the porky. The pain in his mouth remained, however, and as his panic had ebbed, he had spent increasing amounts of time attempting to rid himself of the quills. As a result, many had already worked their way deeply into the muscles of his chest and into his throat and mouth. Grotesque swelling of his tongue now added to the difficulty he experienced when closing his mouth, yet he wagged his tail feebly as the gray bitch licked his ears and muzzle.

The pups were hungry, and continued to lick the muzzles of their mother and her mate, and failing to get them to disgorge a meal, they turned their attention to the two buff-colored males but with no better results. The pack had eaten little during the day, and with their efforts unrewarded, the pups could do little but whine impatiently for the meal they would do without. The stench of rotting fish did little to subdue their desire to eat, for it was still present on all of the wolves.

The pack rested for several hours on the nursery meadow, and a weak quarter-moon rode the cloudless sky as the black male shifted quietly in his sleep. The night was devoid of sound and, once more, windless. Only the dream-induced whimperings of the pack leader and the stricken pup intruded on the stillness. A dense layer of fog once more blanketed the meadow, and it was colder than it had been during the previous night. As a result, the pups edged closer to the gray bitch.

Shortly before midnight, the old female sat up to yawn and lick idly at her gimped leg. Her warm breath floated visibly in the dampness of the cold air as she stood and stretched. Several slow steps carried her to the edge of the deep grass, where she squatted to empty her bladder. Then, as she scratched deeply in the soft moss, her ears picked up the almost indiscernible sound of a small airplane approaching from the north.

As the pulsating beat of the craft's engine grew, the gray bitch felt the faint sound vibrations with her legs and feet. Wide awake now, she shivered with the strange nervousness that she felt each time the planes passed overhead. The sensation was not shared by her mate, who merely drew his legs closer to his body before resuming his sleep.

Moving farther back beneath the dark spruces, the bitch pitched her ears forward as she attempted to pinpoint the direction from which the droning sound came. Though she could not consciously recall it, the event which had resulted in the crippling of her leg had become an inseparable part of the sound she now feared more than any other.

It had been cold, excruciatingly so, during her second winter of life. Each day, high winds had ripped ragged patches of snow from ridgetops and broad openings among the stunted spruce of the high country. She had been whelped in a dry, gully-like side spur of Yanert Fork more than fifty miles to the southeast of the St. George Creek den site. The den of her birth had been a new one for her parents when they took up residence there during that spring eleven years before. The litter of which she was part had consisted of only three pups, one of which had died of respiratory illness before its eyes had fully opened.

During the months that followed, both the small gray bitch and her larger dun-colored brother had received a doting period of rearing in the absence of other littermates. Their sire had been an old wolf, and the litter into which the pair had been whelped would have been his last, even had he not become the victim of a steel trap cleverly placed among the scattered and stripped bones of a moose kill during the winter which followed their birth. His screams paralyzed his mate and the two pups, after which they panicked and broke, racing wildly into the snow-laden brush adjacent to the kill, scattering as they ran.

Much later, as the three wolves found each other more than two miles away, they were still confused and badly frightened. As a result, they moved even higher among the slopes above the kill and spent the following night lying up in the lea of a rocky shale outcropping. The following morning was spent carefully approaching the kill. The old female chose a slow, zigzag route, backtracking often, and pausing for long periods of time to test the cold air that moved upslope. The two pups whined softly as they followed the bitch, confused as she was by the absence of their father and reluctant to return to the site of the old kill, a place they had visited often during the week just past.

The feeble noon sun had done little to warm the windblown clearing as the three wolves found it. After several false starts, the old bitch stood nose to nose with her mate as he crouched on his belly among the rib bones of the kill. His shivering body covered the trap that held his hind leg securely, and he whined low in his throat as his mate licked his muzzle.

The old female and her two pups spent several days nearby before hunger finally drove them away, for even the cold-dried hide scraps at the kill had been eaten. Two days after their departure the old male died, his strength sapped by almost a week spent fighting both the trap that held him and the blue cold of the still long nights. The three wolves survived what remained of the winter by sheer luck and a total dependence upon a population of snowshoe hares that numbered in the millions along the slopes of the Alaska Range.

The spring of the following year came early, and with the creeks running bank-full once more, the three wolves began an intermittent trek that eventually ended near the Wood River, a watercourse that would later represent the eastern boundary of the vast territory eventually claimed by the gray bitch's brother. The trio wintered along the Wood, once more content to survive upon the still-plentiful hares and the carcasses of those that had already died as the population inexorably began its rapid decline. It was during the following spring, the second of her life, that the gray female pup learned about airplanes.

Sunshine had flooded the low hills where she rested with her mother. The black pup had wandered off earlier on one of his many seemingly aimless junkets. The two wolves dozed in a lethargy of warmth and blinding light as the first chucklings of sound reached their ears. It was a sound that she would learn by hard experience to associate with the countless small airplanes that would pass over her world during her life, but at the time it meant little to her. Like her mother, she sat upright seeking after the source of the sound with her nose and ears until it was far too late.

Both wolves stood as the flickering shadow of the plane swept swiftly over the sunlit snow, its engine idling gently and its slipstream hissing in the still air. Moments before the sun became obliterated, the muffled report of the shotgun startled the female pup, and she trotted quickly to the head of a nearby brush-choked gully where she stopped to look back, her eyes still dazzled by the white sunshine. Following the sound of the plane as its engine roared to life, she watched it climb away steeply.

Mesmerized by the droning sounds of the airplane, she remained at the foot of the small gully as it turned tightly on one down-tipped wing, and its engine gentled once more. This time, because it came from a direction that was away from the glaring sun, she watched intently as the plane approached for the second time. Once more, she heard the deceptively muffled explosion of the gun, but even before she heard it and was engulfed by the plane's racing shadow, she was hurled violently sideways into the brushy willows and buried beneath the dry snow that cascaded downward from their crowns.

White-hot needles of pain stabbed upward into her right hip as she ascended into the dubious protection afforded by the shallow gully. A pink smear now showed in each of the wide-spaced track clusters she left behind as, panting heavily, she reached the gully's upper end. Here she paused only long enough to bite at her hind leg before continuing at a broken trot across a broad snow-covered shale field which led to a jumble of boulders at the foot of an ancient rock-slide. Here she stopped to watch her back trail and lick at the nagging pain in her hind leg.

Had the gray bitch been closer, she would have learned even more about shadows which engulf young wolves with discordant sound. She could have watched the plane as it landed lightly on its skis. She might also have watched the man who waded through the deep snow to retrieve the dead body of her mother. As it was, she heard only the distance-weakened sounds of the departing plane as she slipped away into the vastness of snow-drifted broken rock.

A single buckshot pellet had punctured the fleshy part of her upper leg and then coursed downward just beneath the skin before exiting along the side of her foot. Tendons had been torn as it passed, but little bleeding had occurred, and though the wound's throbbing pain caused her to whimper and stretch her neck as the spasms passed, she would survive. She would do so, however, bearing a permanent limp, a defect that would handicap her existence and very probably accelerate the simple process of growing old. Even the big black pup seemed to sense the gravity of the wound as the pair were reunited just before darkness once more cloaked the high country, and he too licked the pale red stains on his sister's hind leg.

The long-legged hares that had kept the pups alive during their first winter provided two vital functions during their second. Again they existed as a fairly dependable source of food, but more importantly, their presence and familiarity provided a mechanism which made learning to hunt on their own possible for both pups. As the snows of winter once more decayed, the pups were able to bring a caribou to earth, the first they had ever killed. Shortly thereafter, the gray female felt the first proddings of her initial period of heat. The breeding which followed between herself and the black wolf seeded the first of many pregnancies which produced healthy offspring despite the blood ties the two shared.

Perhaps because of the passing plane, the black leader was also on his feet, stretching his long legs and yawning luxuriously. The two buff males followed his lead, and soon the entire pack was forming up and preparing to move on. The gray bitch nosed her injured pup as she joined the group, the plane forgotten as quickly as it had intruded into her consciousness, and she swung in next to the black as the pack moved into the spruces.

The route selected by the black wolf carried toward the mountains, and after only a few hours of travel the pale lemon light of another dawn tipped the trees, changing them from black to deep green.

CHAPTER 10

There were a dozen caribou in the small band that had bedded among the red-leafed willow where Chicken Creek slipped unobtrusively through a series of small tundra clearings on the first slopes beneath the Japan Hills. The itinerant group was made up entirely of Roman-nosed cows and their several calves of the year. Even in the almost total darkness of the wet, cloud-mantled night, the whitish hair coats of the calves made them luminously visible on the open hillside.

Part of the Delta Herd, the fragmentary group had broken from the main body of animals to range among the lower slopes of the mountains during the final weeks of summer. The parent herd, numbering about two thousand animals, was at best an unstable entity. Overhunting by man and wolves had created a status quo which had inevitably resulted in an over-all decline in herd growth.

The falling rain, though absorbed blotterlike by the parched tundra, collected on the dense coats of the resting cows, and dripped steadily from their spindly, asymmetric antlers. Motionless and bunched as they were in the small, spruce-bordered clearing, they resembled nothing more than a collection of embedded boulders in the dark softness of moss, though an almost invisible layer of steam, produced by their breathing and the wet warmness of their bodies, hung over them.

After leaving the nursery meadow, the black male and the nine wolves that followed him had recrossed Fish Creek at a broad gravelly shallows. Later they reached and crossed both St. George and Gold King creeks, moving steadily eastward.

During the day the wind had gusted continuously, then died during late afternoon. A dense layer of high clouds had moved from the southeast to slowly obscure the pale early autumn sky, and by evening the overcast had lowered to produce a cold rain, which now dripped steadily among the gnarled spruces and underbrush along the dry bed of Chicken Creek.

The black shook water from his sodden coat in the rapidly waning light beneath the trees. During the week that had followed the wolves' departure from the nursery meadow, he had become less content with idleness and had initiated the pack's nocturnal travels earlier each day. The restlessness he felt was accentuated by the rain that fell during the evening that the pack reached Chicken Creek.

The night was water soaked and quiet, the patterings of raindrops on the rocks and gravel of the nearby creekbed audible as a hushed whispering, punctuated irregularly by the sounds of heavier drops that collected among the tips of cone-laden spruce branches before falling to earth.

The gray bitch's pup continued to suffer terribly. His mouth and lips were now swollen to ugly proportions and his tongue was dried and cracked where it protruded from his half-closed jaws. Infection, which began almost immediately, had become aggravated as the quills worked into the muscles of his jaws and the soft tissues of his mouth and throat. The seepage of blood had stopped, to be replaced by the drainings of the infection itself, and the pup had become listless, his glazed eyes vacant of expression. Because he could not eat, the fast during the week following the pack's departure from the nursery meadow had produced visible effects upon him. Even though he became excited by the warm scent of fresh food after each rabbit was killed, he was unable to eat any of the stringy flesh.

The black, upon reaching the bed of Chicken Creek, moved sporadically and without real purpose as he passed through the oppressive envelope of wet darkness. The pack was moving in a southerly direction now, gradually climbing the grade formed by the creekbed itself, its members picking their way slowly among the rocks and debris that had collected during the spring before. Even then Chicken Creek was unimpressive, existing only as a moderate trickle of whiskey-colored water, seemingly unaffected by the surges that helped raise the level of the Wood. The bed offered, at best, a relatively unobstructed path, but the wolves used it.

Even in the almost total absence of light, the creekbed appeared as a tunnel of vague gray outlines to the wolves, and the big black followed its course easily. His coat, like those of the others, was flat-streaked with the rain, and he shook himself repeatedly while pausing to investigate invisible pockets of scent among the wet rocks and beneath the dripping cutbanks.

Ahead of the gray bitch, the big wolf continued his erratic pace. Moving through a narrow cut in a low ridge where the creekbed was constricted in a series of boulder-laced steps and shallow pools of stagnant water, he watched a short-tailed weasel bound snakelike over the rocks ahead before disappearing into a jungle of hanging rootlets beneath the streambank. The big wolf took little interest in the ribbon of bitter gland scent that the little predator left behind, its potency somehow repugnant to his sensitive nose.

The old bitch followed closely at her mate's heels as he

clawed his way up the final wall of slippery rocks and drift-
wood at the ravine's head. Then, at the precise moment he
was about to arch his back and shake the water from his
coat once more, he walked into the invisible wall of warm
scent.

The heavy odor of caribou ran downslope, layered and
held close to the ground by the cold stillness of rain-washed
air. Even here, a half mile below the clearing where the animals rested, the creekbed collected it. Where only moments
before the black wolf's nose had detected only the remnants
of the weasel, it was now filled with the pleasantness of wet
caribou hair, droppings, and the mild fermenting pungency
of exhaled breath.

The pack quickly gathered around the black wolf to stand
nose to nose. Then, sampling the air, they moved in circles
on the narrow creekbed with their tails held low and wagging excitedly. There was no question as to the direction
from which the scent came, and after only a brief pause the
wolves swung out of the rocks, angling away from the creek.

Angling upslope and moving single file through the wet
underbrush beneath the band of spruce that bordered the
creekbed, the black moved with renewed purpose. Rain-
water cascaded from the brittle red leaves of ground willow
and dwarf birch to further soak the wolves' coats as they
moved in silence.

Only a short time was required for the big wolf to reach a
position several hundred yards below the clearing occupied
by the band of caribou. Here he stopped, the rest bunching
impatiently behind him. Along with the gray bitch and his
two adult sons, the black tested the slowly moving air that
still flowed toward him from the direction of the small herd.
Then, as if by some mutually arranged plan, the two buff
wolves moved laterally along the slope, still concealed by
willows and short spruces. The three pups followed the two
light-colored female wolves hesitantly, while the injured

pup flopped down among the roots of an upturned tree stump nearby.

Moments after the buff wolves disappeared, the black was followed by his smaller mate as he began to ascend the slope occupied by the caribou. The big male selected a route which took him on a crosswind course, and as the pair moved higher, the scent source weakened perceptibly and was finally lost. The black slowed, casting sideways as he searched to once more pick up the ribbon of odor. Failing in this, he flattened himself in the soggy moss, and the female followed his lead.

The disappearance of scent carried the instinctive hint that the two wolves were now almost above the caribou, though it was not a conscious suggestion. From here, training dictated a slow approach, and the animals covered the next several yards belly-crawling, their ears upright and alert to the small sounds of the night. Finally, moving even more slowly than before, the black stopped once more and cautiously raised his massive head above the dripping vegetation that carpeted the clearing's upper margin.

Downslope, and visible only because of slight head movements, were several sets of dark antlers above the contour of the clearing. The black wagged his tail slowly, its tip brushing his mate's nose. She edged closer to his side. The rain had stopped during their slow approach to their final position, and the ears of both wolves picked up the subtle sounds of movement as the cows shifted their positions among the bog tufts below.

One of the caribou, a gaunt cow among several that occupied the clearing's upper half, stood slowly to shake the rain from her ash-colored back. Then, reaching forward with a blunt hind hoof, she jabbed several times at her upper shoulder in a halfhearted attempt to relieve the itching produced by one of the many warble fly larvae that lived beneath the skin of her back. The inch-long wormlike grubs of

the warble were part of a new crop she would support until
the following spring. Each had developed from tiny eggs
laid on the cow's legs and flanks during the summer just
past. These eggs then produced tiny larvae which had migrated to the skin of her back and burrowed beneath her
thick hide. At winter's end, the larvae would enlarge the
holes through which they entered, fall onto the ground, and
become adult flies. The cycle would then begin anew.

Seemingly satisfied, the old cow belched deeply, then
stood staring downslope into the darkness of the hillside,
blissfully unaware of the presence of the two wolves that
had now closed the distance between them to less than fifty
yards.

Both the black and his mate were motionless now, flat on
their steaming bellies, and watching the cow. As they studied her, another caribou rose from the ground and, like the
first, shook herself. Now there was general movement
among the cows, as each in turn rose from her bed in the
wet moss. An invisible flutter of unrest had been transmitted
from one animal to the next, though the caribou had neither
seen nor winded the stalking wolves. The calves were the
last to mimic the movements of the adults.

The first weak light of false dawn was filtering through
the overcast as the big black felt the wind with his broad
nose one last time. Then he bunched his powerful hind legs
under his belly and hitched his body forward. The coolness
that ran along the side of his muzzle was an almost
undefined reminder that the air currents on the slope still favored his position. Now, however, the time for watching was
over, and with a quick glance over his shoulder at his mate,
he launched himself from concealment.

Both wolves erupted from their vantage point running flat
to the ground, tails held low, and at full speed. Little sound
attended the charge as they hurtled downslope into the caribou. During the first fleeting seconds, the gray bitch veered

away at a slight angle, her fifteen-foot leaps eating up the distance between her and the now lunging caribou. Both gravity and surprise were allies of the wolves, and placed the caribou at a critical disadvantage.

The small tundra clearing became a scene of instant bedlam. Within the space of the wolves' first appearance, a chaos of blurred movement had erupted, punctuated by the sounds of clicking hooves, wheezing grunts, and the tearing of wet moss and willow roots as blunt hooves splayed and slashed in the panicked frenzy of attempted escape.

A fleeing calf, its nose held high, bleated in terror as the momentum of the gray bitch's final vaulting leap carried her past the floundering animal, causing the old wolf to miss her best opportunity at a quick kill. Though she recovered instantly, the calf had already switched directions and quickly had the advantage.

The black wolf was luckier. In full stride, he launched his own leap while still ten feet away from a barren cow that had, like the calf, hesitated almost imperceptibly to change direction. The same maneuver that spared the calf spelled doom for the cow as the 140-pound wolf crashed into her rib cage just behind her shoulder. The collision caused her to pitch sideways and stumble.

In a blur of motion too fast to see, the black switched direction, his jaws clamping shut over the cow's muzzle, enveloping it in his mouth. Then, using his bulk and strength as a lever, the big wolf dragged the hapless cow to a stop, forcing her head downward into the soft moss. The black's grip effectively closed off the cow's labored breathing, and though she outweighed her attacker by more than fifty pounds, her inability to inhale caused her to weaken quickly.

Having missed in her own first lunge, the gray bitch cut her pursuit short, and two long bounds carried her to her mate's side. Without pause, she ran her own muzzle beneath the cow's neck where she took a firm grip on its throat. As she did, the cow slowly rolled over on her side, allowing the bitch to slide her jaws forward, thus gaining a fuller grip. Closing powerfully, the gray bitch felt the brittle cartilage of the caribou's windpipe collapse. Minutes later, the cow's eyes rolled and her legs stiffened spasmodically as death came by suffocation.

During the first few moments of the black wolf's charge, his two sons lay in ambush below the clearing and directly in the path of the fleeing caribou. From their own point of concealment, it had been easy to quickly kill a calf that almost overran them, even without the belated aid of the white bitches.

An eerie silence once more settled over the clearing, and only the hoof clicks and blowing snorts of escaping caribou drifted back from the dark spruces below the clearing. The cold rain resumed as the wolves fed, and as they did, the dun pup could only whimper as he made feeble attempts to tear at the hide-stripped hindquarters of a calf, after which he circled the feeding buff males, whining in frustration and renewed pain. Though they had followed the stalking pack and had scented the caribou, the presence of the three remaining pups was motivated more by simple curiosity than by any awareness of the events which were about to occur. As yet, they knew little about hunting, a fact that was inconsistent with their burgeoning size. Then, with the sudden initiation of the attack by their parents, followed by the confusion of fleeing prey, the pups had scattered among the lunging caribou, dodging quickly away from the shadowy forms that flickered among the rain-drenched dwarf spruce of the hillside. Curiosity had quickly given way to fear, a more basic reaction, one which, until now, they had been relative strangers to.

The wolves remained on the clearing adjacent to Chicken Creek for three days before moving on toward the higher slopes of the range. The carcasses of both caribou lay stripped of all but a few tendons and the cartilage around knee joints and sternum. Leg bones lay scattered among torn bits of hair-covered hide, and the moss was packed flat in the vicinity of both kills. After gorging during the first morning, the pack had eaten steadily, its members content to doze when not trotting the short distance to nearby seeps for water.

Suffocating clouds of mosquitoes that descended upon the feeding wolves, especially during the hours of daylight, made even the act of eating a painful exercise in frustration. At such times the pack fed sporadically, the wolves attempting to escape their puny tormentors by dragging parts of the caribou away from the kill. In the end, however, such efforts provided less relief than did big forefeet used to wipe away the insects that coated muzzles and eyes. There was, in fact, no escape except that provided by the cooling air of evening. With relief came deep sleep, which, in itself, attested to the exhaustion caused by the bloodsucking insects.

Following the kill, the rain continued, then cold, blustering winds mixed with white sleet. Later the sun shone once more, but the air was colder, and when the black wolf led his followers away, the pack was only nine strong, for the big dun-colored male pup had died. In the presence of plenty, he had starved, the infection and cold wetness serving only to hurry the inevitable result of his encounter with the porcupine. The gray bitch had made numerous attempts to feed him, but even her pawing eventually failed to make him rise to his feet, and the rasping sigh of his dying caused her to sniff disinterestedly at his emaciated body, after which she trotted away.

There would be little to come back to, but the wolves would return to the Chicken Creek kill, as was their habit. It would merely be a token visit, however, for the ravens that had lived with the pack at the kill took full possession even as the last wolf disappeared from sight. The body of the pup, made pathetic by the rain which had flattened its dun fur, would be a bounty, for the broad-beaked scavengers drew few distinctions in what they consumed.

❧ CHAPTER 11

Like spring, the Arctic autumn is a time of transition destined to end almost before it begins. Even during early August, while temperatures of midsummer had still wrapped the great flats of interior Alaska in warmth, subtle changes were occurring that bespoke the brevity of winter's absence from the land.

In addition to the more obvious foreshortening of days that had recently gone without total darkness, most of the aspens that flanked the low hills had suddenly changed to brilliant gold, their leaves fluttering conspicuously in a sea of lush green spruce, and tissue-thin curls of bark glittered brightly along white birch trunks as they became backlighted by the sun. Then, with the swift passage of a few additional weeks, the transition reached its zenith as leaves wrinkled and then tumbled to earth, to become windrowed along creekbeds and layered thickly in still ponds, like chaff from a brief harvest.

Concurrent with the rapid cessation of growth that had gone almost unchecked for less than three months, the land lost still more of its moisture. The supply of water stored by the powdery soil had been spent lavishly in the normal absence of summer rain, and, perhaps, at no other time during

the year did the Arctic resemble a true desert, which in fact
it is.

With the early autumn drought, rivers lost still more of
the levels they had retained, while ponds and sloughs withered visibly. Glacial runoff lost much of the brown silt and
cleared as its own supply decreased under the influence of
freezing nighttime temperatures. Finally, like great healing
wounds, the high ice fields coagulated, their flow stopping
completely except during the few short hours of sun that
each day still provided.

A multitude of other changes existed as lesser products of
the entire process. The great, suffocating swarms of insects—
mosquitoes, gnats, flies, and others—that had been born suddenly in the water-swollen spring died and disappeared as
autumn matured. Only their eggs and larvae remained as an
unseen part of the patient scheme that would now wait
three fourths of a year for redefinition.

By late August, waterfowl, newly arrived a little less than
two months before, had produced young that were already
flying on adult wings. They too had relied upon the abun-
dance of summer water for generation, and finally, upon
their precocious ability to fly, would escape to places that
would guarantee more water throughout the rest of the
year.

The massive lower peaks of the Alaska Range were the
first to whiten with snow, and by early September even the
higher foothills were covered with thin mantles of it. At first,
the dusting of snow at the lower elevations quickly disappeared under the effect of daylight, leaving the dark ridges
veined with white, but by October, as the lengthening
nights began to outlast the shortening days, snow once more
became a permanent part of the far horizon.

During the weeks that followed the pack's departure from
the nursery meadow on the flats, a cold wind rolled over the
foothills of the mountains, hissing among the dry, needle-

laden spruce boughs and swirling the dead leaves in waterless tundra-bordered creekbeds. In shadowed places, untouched by the lowering sun, water which had outlasted the advance of autumn froze, and finally, as the seeps dried beneath the new ice, only hollow shells remained.

In his travels, the black wolf broke through many such places, as had the others. The gray bitch's pups had, at first, been confused as they skidded and fell on the black ice. Then, as they learned the short-stepping gait required in negotiating it, their confidence grew. Rocking up on their hind legs, they took to thrusting stiff-legged with their front feet, challenging its presence and experimenting with its form. It was their first encounter with ice in any real quantity, and they seized upon each opportunity to explore its texture as they traveled with the adults.

During the first days of October, the St. George Creek pack moved into the obscure drainage of Three-Mile Creek. Though the wolves had traveled steadily during each day, the black had followed an erratic course. Finally, the ponderous wall of peaks thrust upward steeply above the pack as it crossed through the last broken gullies and spruce thickets where the Wood River emerged from the range. From there it had been but a short distance to Three-Mile Creek.

The big wolf and his mate knew the place well. Probably due to some underground spring, water trickled among the rocks of the tiny creek until well after the arrival of cold weather. Three-Mile Creek was but one more watercourse which fed the Wood from within the mountains, and to reach it the pack had traversed the open tundra slopes in the steep valley of the bigger river.

The gray bitch's pups were now more than half grown, and lingering juvenile traits had, for the most part, disappeared. The two blue-gray males each weighed more than fifty pounds, while the light-gray female remained smaller.

The thin wool of rust-colored puppy hair had been shed and then replaced by the long guard hairs of the adult wolf. With the new hair coats, the male pups assumed an even darker hue, and except for his great size, resembled their father closely. The female, on the other hand, had grown even lighter in color, her flanks and hips tinged with traces of ocher. She was identical to her dam.

Each of the pups had lost most of the gangling clumsiness of immaturity. Their legs, once too long for the younger bodies they supported, were now proportional to the musculature of the adult wolf. Paws that had looked oversized still retained their appearance, but had become knobbier with the thickening of tendons and cartilage joints.

Perhaps most prominent of all the changes the pups had undergone was found in their new hair coats. Each now wore the long shoulder ruff and roach hairs of the full-grown wolf, and, as a result, they had assumed the massive bulk of adult wolves in their forequarters and necks. The long guard hairs of the males were blue-gray, tipped with black, and underlaid with a thickening base of fine shorter fur that would insulate when the weather demanded.

Puppy, or milk, teeth had been lost during mid-September as the young wolves reached the age of four months. The needlelike, shallow-rooted teeth had disappeared without pain or even notice during countless chewing sessions on virtually any object that had come to the pups' attention. The replacement of these teeth by their adult counterparts was an orderly but gradual process which saw canines, molars, and the rest lost and then regained in pairs.

Finally, muzzles, once pugged and short, had lengthened and were backed now by broader foreheads and the wide-set yellow-amber eyes characteristic of adult wolves.

As a result of these changes, the nine wolves that slipped quietly into the inclined bed of Three-Mile Creek were, in appearance, adult wolves. No longer was the presence of the gray bitch's pups emphasized by their appearance or behavior. Though they still played, their games had taken on more sophisticated dimensions as reckless tumbling became what appeared to be planned ambush as the young wolves stalked each other patiently. Superficially, such games were the product of a simple need to expend energy, but in fact they held more useful meaning. The attacks from concealment served the purpose of teaching each pup the rudiments of stalking prey while allowing for a continued expression of status among the three. Consistent success redefined dominance of victor over vanquished, though such attacks never ended in more than a tumbling collision after which the pup that had initiated the attack stood over its victim, who inevitably rolled over on its back in submission. The small gray female pup was, more often than not, a victim.

The steep drainage of Three-Mile Creek was yet another nursery site that the black wolf and his mate had used during other years. On a mossy incline subtended by a badly eroded shelf of loose rock, bleached droppings left by the wolves were scattered among the gray lichens and moss hummocks. In addition, vague trails radiated from the bench into nearby rock piles and side gullies.

The site offered an excellent vantage point from which the wolves could watch the meandering creekbed below as it threaded its way toward the upper valley of the Wood River. The pups accepted the place for what it was, having by now lost most of the apprehension they felt when first left alone by the pack as it hunted. It was but one more sign of their growing maturity.

The black male traveled alone on several nights during the first week of the pack's stay at Three-Mile Creek. Usually splitting from the rest after the wolves had traveled some distance from the nursery site, he occupied himself with the idle pastime of mousing among the skeletal buildings of an abandoned placer camp higher in the broad valley of the Wood. Though in reality his efforts went largely unrewarded, he seemed intrigued by the almost unnoticeable scent of creosote which lingered among the porous, dry-rotted timbers and boards left behind by the anonymous humans that once occupied the place. In a caved-in shed near the upper edge of the cluster of debris that was once an orderly group of squat buildings, he sought out and rolled luxuriously in earth still saturated with old engine oil that once seeped from a power generator.

The big male's return to the Three-Mile Creek site was always cause for exaggerated celebration, as the rest of the pack crowded close to shoulder him and nuzzle his snout. The big wolf accepted such gestures as his due, but the wagging of his tail signaled his own enjoyment of the ritual.

If one were allowed the luxury of assumption, it could be said that the swiftly passing weeks of late September and early October represented the ideal in contented comfort for the St. George Creek pack. Tundra insects were virtually absent except during midday, when remnant skeins of gnats hovered over the sleeping pack. The autumn air was clean and cool beneath a high vault of pale-blue sky, and the rain showers of earlier weeks became less frequent as winter approached.

For the gray bitch, autumn brought a continued relaxation of the daily responsibilities she felt for her pups. Though she still disgorged food for them upon returning from her nightly travels, even this necessity was gradually changing with their growing preference for the pieces and bones brought to them by the pack. The wolves had managed to kill two more caribou, one coming quickly upon the heels of the good fortune at Chicken Creek, and the other a week later. They returned to both carcasses for several days, before leaving the most recent half-consumed, and hunting elsewhere.

The wolves frequented the high nursery site until mid-

October. Then, one afternoon under an overcast sky, the two buff males grew restless and, after several false starts, set out down the slope trotting slowly, their coats flattening under a cold gusting wind. The black watched them from his vantage point above the mossy bench until they were almost out of sight. Then he too rose, shook his coat, and, with the rest of the pack in tow, followed his sons down the mountain.

What was left of the afternoon slipped by quickly as the pack picked its way down the steep incline of Three-Mile Creek to the valley of the Wood. The wolves arrived along the bigger stream just as the broad gravel bars of the river were plunged into deep shadow, the sun having spent itself behind the high peaks. The black paused to watch a flock of clucking ptarmigan where they fed unhurried among the short willows on the far bank. After wading into the shallow current in a halfhearted attempt to get closer to the white-speckled birds, he returned to the pack before starting downstream.

The bed of the Wood widened perceptibly as the pack neared the place where it left the mountains. Here, after wading the river, the black wolf swung upward on a mossy slope, seeking a well-used sheep trail that meandered westward along the base of the range. Finding it, he quickened his pace, trotting easily in the powdery dust of the deep-cut trail.

The pack had used the route often in past times, and a sliver of moon rode the sky where it darkened and lost the salmon translucence of late evening. The wind had once more blown itself out, and in the gathering darkness, calm once more settled over the foothills. The wolves moved in silence, and were only vague shadows as they reached Bonnifield Creek, twelve miles from the nursery site. Above them, in the jumbled rocks of the drainage, lay the remains of their most recent kill. Because the weather was still warm enough to have caused what remained of the caribou to go sour, the black wolf found the carcass easily in total darkness.

The caribou, a young bull with three-foot antlers bearing ragged streamers of shedding velvet, had been obtained by the pack through the simple expedient of entrapment. In its upper reaches, Bonnifield Creek passed through a series of steep-walled crevices, too sheer even for the sure-footed Dall sheep to scale. The wolves had negotiated the steep bed of the creek with the wind blowing from behind and up the drainage. As a result, their scent had reached the small group of bulls that was bedded among the rocks before the pack detected its presence.

The gray bitch had collided with her big mate from the rear as he stopped suddenly, listening to the clatter of stones and rock that came from the drainage ahead. Then the band of caribou had exploded into the open, scattering as, still trying to pinpoint its scent, they spotted and nearly collided with the pack. There had been no time for an organized charge, and the black made a spontaneous but ineffective attempt to head off the nearest bull. Then, cut off by the gray bitch, the last caribou to exit the narrow ravine skidded to a stop in the soft gravel, spun in his tracks, and lunged back toward the dubious safety of the gully. The black and his sons swung behind, and the bull's doom was effectively sealed, as he climbed the steep ravine floor, where gravity once more became a deadly disadvantage.

The caribou's panicked flight back into the narrow confines of the drainage covered less than a quarter mile. Then, eyes bulging and panting visibly, he attempted to scale a low rocky outcrop that barred his path, a place where a small waterfall had tumbled during spring. As his blunt hooves fought for purchase, exhaustion caused him to stumble, the rock tearing great gouts of hollow hair from his brisket and belly.

Had the wolves been close enough, the fall would have given them the opportunity to engage the bull. As it was, the caribou had enough time to turn, and with his sides heaving spasmodically, he faced the black wolf and his mate.

In the confined silence, only the panting of caribou and wolves and the occasional sounds made by dislodged gravel intruded upon the standoff in the ravine. The pack leader and his sons were content to flop down below the bull as he stood straddle-legged and facing them. Minutes passed slowly. Then the caribou made his second mistake, and this one killed him.

Still exhausted, the bull attempted to break through the waiting wolves in a desperate attempt to retrace his route back down the drainage. He lunged between the black and his sons, stumbling among the rocks as tired muscle and tendon failed to respond. Though he remained on his feet, he felt the big male's teeth as they found the tightness of his belly just ahead of his hind quarters. At the same moment, one of the buff males launched his own attack from above and behind the bull's pistoning hind legs, his lunge carrying him well onto the bull's back, where his jaws locked on the loose skin above the caribou's shoulders.

Even before the tan wolf's ninety-five pounds caused the bull to stumble one last time and fall headlong into the fragmented rock, and break one antler from its pedicel attachment in the skull, his intestines had already surged through his torn belly.

The bull's hind legs still jerked spasmodically with his dying as the black wolf began to feed on the bluish loops of gut. He growled deeply at his mate and her sons, but they ignored the threat. The single resident female that had accompanied the pack hung well below the rest, seeming content to wait her turn at the meat. Her sister had remained at Three-Mile Creek with the gray bitch's pups. The following day had seen the entire pack at the kill on Bonnifield Creek.

The night of the pack's final visit to the Bonnifield kill passed slowly, and in the hours of darkness, frost built on the rocks of the ravine. It remained untouched by the lightening dawn sky framed in the high rim of the peaks above as the gray bitch stirred and tested the air with her nose. The black and his sons dozed nearby, shivering involuntarily as the old female licked her chest and forequarters. Finally, yawning deeply, she stood slowly, stretching her legs to rid them of their cold-induced stiffness.

The pups slept close to one another near the stripped and partially antlered head of the caribou. It was perhaps because of their presence at the kill that the pack did not travel during the day which followed, its members content to rest nearby. Later, as the shadows of early afternoon again chilled the ravine's floor, the gray bitch once more raised her head to watch the others. Tucked beneath her, her lame hind leg had grown stiff with the long period of idleness, and she listened disinterestedly to the low-pitched rumble of a passenger jet high overhead as it let down for a landing at Fairbanks, seventy land miles to the north.

The old female nipped at her gimped leg. She had seen many of the big planes that passed regularly above the flats, and their sound had become commonplace. Probably because the sounds they made were unlike the small planes she feared, she ignored them.

Somewhere, higher in the drainage where it forked before losing itself in the shifting foot of a vast shale slide, a marmot whistled shrilly, its call echoing hollowly in the deep ravine. The gray bitch's ears twitched with the sound. Then, standing, she once more stretched her hind legs and scratched her thin neck, her movements causing a single raven to pause in its picking among the leftovers before cocking its head and taking wing.

Several pikas, small soft-furred rodents that lived among

the jumbled rocks, busied themselves in the fissures above the wolves. They had spent the day tirelessly gathering the dry sedges that grew sparsely in the drainage, then storing them in tiny haystacks among the rocks. Called rock rabbits by the sourdoughs, they relied upon such stores during the winter, for unlike the spotted parka squirrels that were their neighbors of the lower slopes, they did not hibernate.

Another autumn evening had deepened the blue shadows in the ravines as the wolves descended to the mouth of Bonnifield Creek, and once more followed the big black along the network of sheep trails that led to the west. The faint musk of dead leaves and spruce pitch wafted momentarily over the slopes from the flats below, and was then replaced by the more sterile and slightly warmer air that descended from above. Unseen by the wolves because they were pitched behind the lower ridges, the peaks of the Alaska Range jutted in pink light, reflecting what remained of the sunset.

CHAPTER 12

The little plane passed some distance from the wolves as they descended Bonnifield Creek. Well out over the flats, it was silhouetted against the peach-tinted sky as an almost indiscernible moving dot. Only the gray bitch paused to look for it, but it escaped her eyes, hidden by distance and the deepening dusk.

Soft red light radiating from the luminous needles and gauge faces of the airplane's instrument panel reflected on white beard stubble and the deep creases and crow's feet in the pilot's face. Thick, rimless glasses bridged his nose and a faded knit cap topped his balding head. With the lap belt loosened, he sat easy in the front seat of the two-place, fabric-skinned craft, only subconsciously aware of the mild smells of warm oil emanating from the engine and the gasoline that filled the wings. The plane's patched skin, faded red paint, and the dents which pocked the leading edge of the wings would have appeared shoddy in the charge of someone younger. As it was, the plane, like the man, was old and tired, the result of the accumulation of long years in this land of cold winters.

At sixty-seven, Jake Tatum was a bitter, lonely man. He guided the plane westward by simple habit, his right thumb and calloused forefinger feeding minute automatic pressures to the control stick which stubbed between his knees. The cool smoothness of the evening air over the flats behind the plane's tail continued as he flew two thousand feet above the deceptive gentleness of rolling foothills.

After a late departure from Fairbanks and having crossed the flats, the old man had picked up and followed the looping course of the Wood River almost to its deep valley in the hills before swinging the plane's nose to the west and behind the Japan Hills. There was little to see beneath the plane's belly, only the crevices made by the creeks that wrinkled the contour of the land as they wandered outward onto the flats, but had there been a need to do so, he could have instantly identified the Bonnifield drainage as it slipped beneath the plane's left wing tip, ten miles to the south.

Tatum had spent the entirety of his adult life in the Arctic, first in the raw territory and finally in the new state. When he was new to the big land, youth had imparted its boundless optimism and made acceptance of the rapid changes occurring there seem trivial. As a result, he had ignored them until advancing age forced his attention. By then, it seemed to Tatum, it had been too late.

Only the gut-cramping realization that the best parts of his life had slipped away while he coped with his chosen life-style brought such changes to his attention, and the panic of easily counted remaining years magnified them to breathless proportions. Finally, the squirming realization that life was finite, even for him, had been replaced by an obstinate bitterness as he recounted the forces that had seemingly accumulated overnight to crowd him out.

With few exceptions, the restrictions upon his simple activities always seemed to relate directly to the increasing crowds of newcomers, the Cheechakos. That he once had fallen into the same category mattered little, the very size and remoteness of the unpeopled territory having neutralized the significance of his own arrival here. He had desired only to see the land, taking from it just enough to get by and content with the fact that he neither expected nor wanted to get rich. Only the prospectors and others who sought gold had what Tatum looked upon as greedy motivation, and he had shook his head and chuckled at the hardships such men endured. At the time, only their scattered presence made them somehow amusing and deceptively insignificant.

Then somebody discovered oil on the north slope of the distant Brooks Mountain Range, and the activities of men who looked for money in the permafrost took on new meaning, even to Tatum. Just after the death of his wife, Dolly, a full-blooded Athabascan Indian, Tatum watched as the land became flooded with pointy-toed, high-living Oklahomans and Texans, all of them wanting into the biggest game in town. Nearing sixty years of age, and having just gotten used to the immutable fact that his own death would rob him of his beloved life-style before he was ready for such a loss, the coming of what others called "the new Alaskans" had, for Tatum, turned distaste to bitterness.

The Lycoming engine in the plane's nose droned smoothly, its sound lost among the carpet of the spruce below, as the old man's hand left the rubber stick grip to absentmindedly pluck a cigarette from the crumpled pack that rested on the ledge above the vibrating instrument panel. Inhaling deeply, he opened the sliding Plexiglas next to his left shoulder slightly, and felt the powerful slipstream suck the dead match from his fingers.

Where once the act of flying had produced welcome isolation from the intrusion of progress, even this was diluted now by an unwanted need to consider bigger things. Though hard to define, it was this single loss of privacy that Tatum resented most.

He had come north when he was sixteen years old. He had never known his mother, and his father, an incorrigible alcoholic, had followed her in death, leaving nothing of any use behind him. The boy, too young to find fault with his lot, traveled from South Dakota to northern Wisconsin, where he had worked for a lumber outfit while living with an aunt. From there, having discovered that he could survive alone, he had hitchhiked to Seattle, and upon his arrival just enough of his earnings were left for a steamship ticket to Seward, Alaska.

During the year preceding his father's death, and in opposition to his drunken objections to the boy's interest in a "rich man's sport," Tatum had learned to fly under the tutelage of a neighbor who had been a paid predator-control agent for the government. Before it ended, Tatum had seen dozens of the gray coyotes the man sought crumple in the withering sheet of pellets thrown by a twelve-gauge shotgun. Then, a year after his arrival in the territory, he had come to the realization that wolves were little different than their smaller cousins, and with the revenue earned as a Gandy dancer during the early construction of the Alaska Railroad line to Fairbanks, he had purchased his first airplane.

During those early years, wolves had been considered vermin by most, sport by some, but never a critter in danger of becoming extinct or even scarce. A clique of pilots emerged whose members gained reputations as wolfers. Most were trappers who refined their skill as pilots to include the hunting of wolves from the dubious security provided by the cramped cockpits of their light planes. Such men usually flew while a companion did the shooting through an open door in the plane's side. A few, like Tatum, learned to do both, but they were rare. The hunting of wolves from airplanes had many aspirants of whom relatively few were ultimately successful, and the planes of those who failed littered the remote places in which they plied the trade, places such as Umiat, Kotzebue, and the river-veined land to the south of the big mountain called McKinley.

As the years passed, wolfing fell from favor among those who learned the folly of bounties, and the monetary value of wolf carcasses virtually collapsed. Many pilots who had once at least paid for the gasoline, ammunition, and repairs to their planes with revenue generated by the sale of wolf pelts dropped out, and only a few had stayed on. Tatum had been one of the latter, and, like the others, had talked himself into believing that his activities were all that stood between survival and desecration of the moose herds in the remoteness of the territory.

That there was some truth to his contention made little difference to the new environmentalists that Tatum and the others became increasingly aware of, and in the end wolfing with airplanes became illegal. Outraged by what he called interference by outsiders, Tatum vowed that he would disregard the new laws, and as he readjusted the plane's course toward the Tatlanika River drainage he smiled inwardly, knowing that, to date, he had kept his promise.

The forty-five-minute flight from Fairbanks to the cabin set deep in the cleftlike valley of the Tatlanika River had been made hundreds of times over the years by the old man. Each time, he subconsciously oriented himself with the tip of the Tanana Hills to the southwest, where they ended abruptly in the hazy distance at the village of Nenana. It was there that his late wife had been born, and it was there that she was buried on the steep hillside above the muddy Tanana.

Dolly had been good for the aging Tatum. Her quiet, almost stoic companionship had stabilized the old man's life for almost eight years. Then, after a long sickness that had been accompanied by more pain than Tatum thought possible, she had died one cold winter night of the cancer that offered no alternatives.

The little sawdust-insulated house that they had shared in Fairbanks had quickly become a prison for the old man, and he had spent what remained of that winter alternating between periods of half-sobriety and a drunken stupor which did little except negate the need to stare out into the gloomy mantle of ice fog that attended the deep cold. Finally, after being cared for by friends, Tatum emerged the following spring, his recovery closely resembling that following a long illness.

Flicking the spent cigarette into the cold air that sucked at the open window, the old man made a minor adjustment in the plane's heading. The vague outlines of the drainage that held the Tatlanika were visible now through the faint blur of the spinning propeller, and he gauged the gathering darkness against his well-practiced ability to land on the poorly defined gravel bar near the cabin.

During the summer and early autumn, the old man had made nearly a dozen trips to the place as he freighted supplies. Groceries, tinned gasoline for the plane, and the balky snowmobile that lay under a needle-spattered tarp beneath the cabin's overhang, traps both spring-loaded and snares, a few bottles of whiskey, and all of the other necessities that practice told him he would need had been cached against the winter ahead. Between trips, he had cut and hauled several cords of twisted spruce from the stands that bordered the river, then cursed his shortness of breath as he wrestled to split it into stove-sized pieces.

The plane's engine gentled as the old man's left hand slipped the throttle lever back, initiating a slow descent into the valley's mouth. The space behind him, where the rear seat had once been attached, was filled with use-blackened traps and a case of canned beans, one of the few luxuries Tatum allowed himself in the weight-restricted task of hauling enough food to last six months. Others relied upon the kindness of their friends who regularly looked after them and air-dropped supplies, but the old man prided himself on making do on his own.

Meat would not be a problem; in fact the young moose he had seen along the gravel spits below the landing strip many times during the weeks past assured it. Killing and hanging the bull would be a priority task now that the old man was almost ready to move in for good.

Tatum hunched forward against the seat belt; his eyes squinted against the gauzy darkness that was settling rapidly in the deeper valley. Then, as the hills that bordered the river's mouth slipped under the plane's belly, he began the one-way approach to the gravel bar. To the right, and unseen, were the remains of a placer mine from which he had robbed enough weathered boards to complete the roof of the cabin almost twenty years before.

Gliding now, the engine chuckling softly, he skillfully adjusted the plane's path along the imaginary line that angled downward to the lower end of the invisible bar. Then, minutes later, the big tires were rattling on the smooth stones, and the plane rolled to a stop.

Only the metallic clicking of the cooling engine and the soft crunch of the old man's shoepacs in the river gravel intruded upon the crisp evening stillness. Standing next to the plane and ahead of the wing, Tatum listened to the small burbling noises made by the river, and they sounded foreign after the ear-numbing drone of the aircraft. As always, the old man savored the quiet. A lifetime of unattached wandering and the solitude he preferred had weakened his capacity for sentimentality, or perhaps had merely replaced it with a galling bitterness produced by the changes he hated. Yet, by the simple device of shutting off the plane's engine and stepping into the quiet isolation of the riverbar, he could dispel the depression that clouded the process of growing old. Because of this, several minutes slipped by before he reluctantly broke the spell by reaching into the plane to slide the twelve-gauge magnum shotgun from its resting place beneath the pile of traps.

The punky ledge of higher ground was welcome as he walked toward the cabin hidden beneath the spruces, for it quieted the harshness of the soft gravel and stones. The vague trail that snaked among the polished root stubs was easy to follow in the darkness, and he smelled the squat log building before its bulk materialized. The yeasty odor made of sweat, the woodsmoke that mahoganied the ridgepole, and the smells of simple meals cooked on the Yukon stove hung tangibly in the cold stillness as he turned a key in the rusty padlock and swung the heavy door inward on its leather hinges.

With years of dependable use, the cabin, like the airplane, had come to assume almost human proportions. Though he owned the tiny house in Fairbanks, his real home was here, primarily because it catered to his growing desire to spend his last years alone.

Full darkness isolated the squat building, and orange lamplight spilled onto the needle-layered ground beneath the single window, as Tatum refilled his enamel cup with bitter coffee. To this he added a dollop of whiskey, then sat at the oilcloth-covered table. Here he found a different kind of solitude. The warmth of the crackling stove and the guttering kerosene lamp produced an island of comfort, a place of escape, and the old man nodded as he stared unseeing into the darkness beyond the circle of weak light. The cabin was a refuge in which even his own voice seemed obtrusive and out of place on the occasions when he talked to himself.

Later, stepping out into the night to empty his bladder, the old man felt the cold pinpricks of snow on his face, and he looked upward as if to pierce the unseen network of spruce boughs that obscured their source. He had seen the wall of cloud that divided the western sky while aloft, and had appraised it correctly, yet he cursed inwardly at the implications that came with the falling snow.

This was his final trip before moving into the cabin on the Tatlanika for the winter. He had planned to stay several days before returning to the city, where he would finish his trivial dealings with creditors, tend to the needs of closing the house, and wait for enough snow to warrant replacement of the plane's big tires with wooden skis. Then he would return with his husky dog and the last of the supplies that would be needed.

Tatum slid the wooden bolt that held the door, and wiped at the moisture that clung to his beard stubble. If the snow fell in enough quantity during the night, he would be forced to leave the next morning, for the plane's wheels were a poor substitute for skis. The thought rankled as fatigue caused him to roll into the blankets on the cabin's single bunk after blowing out the lantern. In the darkness he listened to the scurrying mice as they resumed their secret nighttime travels, and smelled the familiar musk released by the stove's heat from the stacks of pelt stretching boards that hung in the cabin's farthest corner. With it came thoughts of wolves and his long quest for their thick hides along with the reminder that, because they were harder to come by, such pelts were now worth ten times the bounty they once brought. Contemplating this final irony, the old man did not hear the soft collapse of dying ashes in the cooling stove as he dozed and then slept.

CHAPTER 13

The tracks of the St. George Creek pack resembled long intertwined strings of dark beads where they stretched across the barren ground above timberline and to the west of the Gold King Creek headwaters. As they traveled in the darkness, the wolves felt the falling snow as it touched their noses with wet cold and accumulated as droplets of water on the long hair of their shoulders and backs.

The snow was a new experience for the gray bitch's pups. At first confused, they stopped often to shake the snow from their coats and lick its cold residue from their muzzles and forelegs. Then, as the weak grayness of early morning changed the tundra from diffuse gray to shadowless white, they rolled in the thin mantle of powder that covered the frozen ground.

The track patterns of the nine-wolf pack were scattered where the individuals that left them detoured to swing outward on courses parallel to the main direction of travel. Where they rejoined, the impressions of many feet thickened the track to a single column, usually when it became necessary to traverse brush-choked gullies and shallow ravines.

After leaving the Bonnifield drainage and pausing for several hours to investigate a series of rocky escarpments above

Gold King Creek, the big male had once more resumed a westward course, still paralleling the mountains but angling upward until he found open hilltops above the thinning spruces. Here travel was easier, and later, in the shadowless dawn, he descended into the familiar chimneys that jutted high above the St. George Creek drainage.

Little real purpose attended the pack's return to the den meadow, a journey based only in habit patterns which in themselves were unpredictable. The wind-swept bleakness of the place bore little resemblance to the green-carpeted slope the wolves had left behind during the warm autumn, and they sniffed the faint scent that still clung to the den mouth and rocks nearby.

The gray bitch slipped into the hard-frozen darkness of the tunnel, but was not followed by her pups. Below ground and away from the wind, ice flakes rimed the upper curvature of the familiar passageway, ending where the moist warmth of still unfrozen earth reached the cold air from above.

In absolute darkness the old bitch sorted through the age-faded scents that still saturated the powdery cool soil. Satisfied, she quickly returned to the surface, where she was met immediately by the three pups. They frolicked, licked her muzzle, and rolled belly-up before her in a reunion made comic in its proportions by her brief absence.

Moments later, the black nuzzled the gray bitch and then licked her muzzle in a display of affection which, for him, was also somewhat exaggerated. It is doubtful that his attention was catalyzed by the return to the den where the gray bitch's most recent litter was whelped. Only her returning estrus or heat period would once more kindle his desire to copulate, and this annual change was still several months away. Because of the structure of the pack, however, and the fact that the small gray bitch and her huge mate preferred each other, courtship was an ongoing relationship, one which was demonstrated in simple and subtle ways throughout the entire year.

The trickle of black water that once flowed among the rocks nearby had disappeared and St. George Creek had ceased to exist. By midmorning, the anemic light that filtered through a low cloud layer had melted the snow and saturated the moss and dead-leafed willow shrubs with icy water. The pack scattered soon after its arrival, each wolf exploring among the hanging rocks above the meadow for dry places in which to lie up, and the gray bitch paid little attention to the faint pulsating drone made by the unseen red airplane that exited the mountains seven miles to the west.

During the days which followed, heavy clouds continued to obliterate the sky and produce snow during each night as, pushed by the prevailing westerly wind, they gathered and thickened against the peaks and high slopes of the mountains. Then, with the arrival of November, the sodden skies dissipated and the weather grew much colder. In the absence of the overcast, brilliant stars once more glittered in the vast dome of unbroken night sky and the land became stark as the wind hissed among the dead vegetation which carpeted the barren slopes.

The deepening of winter was a process that assumed many forms. Most prominent of all was the inexorable shortening of the days, which seemed to accelerate even more with the deepening of the snow. Below ground in their convoluted burrows, parka squirrels slept in the new dormancy of hibernation, their frantic heart rates and other body processes slowed to a pace more suited for survival during the months of cold darkness that lay ahead.

The grizzly that had summered below the St. George Creek den meadow had left his own meandering tracks in the thin skifts of new snow as he moved hesitantly toward the upper drainage of Hearst Creek. His arrival beneath the obscure undercut shelf of decaying rock where he now slept had come only after several weeks of seemingly aimless wandering as he traversed the ridges between St. George Creek and the broader slopes which formed the eastern half of the Tatlanika River Valley. Only the instinctive urge to travel had sustained the halting journey of more than ten miles.

Before the rapidly shortening days had catalyzed the boar's impatience to find a wintering place, he had spent several weeks among the dense thickets of wild rose and underbrush along the southern margin of the flats. There, as he moved across openings seeking the sweetness of raspberries among the snarled deadfalls, his passage had released great clouds of down-tufted seeds from ripe beds of fireweed. Such places had been frosted with the sun-dried pods of the plant, which, during summer, had painted the clearings a deep violet hue. Brushed by the bear's swaying body and making him sneeze as he inhaled them, millions of tiny airborne seeds floated on the wind, and in their uncounted multitudes assured the next crop.

Later, with the first frosts, the bear had moved to higher ground among the lowest foothills of the range. There he once more grazed with renewed effort upon the starchy, twisted roots of peavine and willow. A patient solidarity of purpose had attended his feeding, and he engaged in it to the exclusion of all other activities.

Finally, high above timberline, he sat childlike during the long afternoons and translucent evenings taking scent from the cool air while scooping frost-wrinkled blueberries from the low, oblong-leafed plants that had produced them and further filling his already distended belly. Attesting to his consuming greed and the cathartic effect of the fruit, his spoors became flaccid and blue-black with partially digested fruit.

During his brief absence from the sleep of winter, the

boar had consumed well over two tons of food, most of it vegetable, during the final half of the short summer. As a result of his voracity, he was a hundred pounds heavier than he had been during the spring, and his body had become roundly opulent with layers of globular yellow fat that blanketed his broad hips and humped back. Then, by mid-November, he had reached the shallow den on Hearst Creek and slept, his slow breathing quickly riming his forepaws and sides with frost.

After staying in the vicinity of the St. George Creek den meadow for almost two days, the pack continued its westward travel, the black staying well up on the broad, treeless ridges that rose and fell while defining the northern side of the Alaska Range. Soon after their departure from the place where the gray bitch's pups had been whelped, the wolves found the deep-cut valley where a dry but major tributary of Fish Creek coursed outward toward the flats. Here they rolled their shoulders and flanks in the droppings of the grizzly, breaking the frost-brittle heaps and scattering the minuscule berry seeds they contained.

The pack's emergence on the long slopes above the Tatlanika River occurred under full darkness and a moonless sky. Without pause, the black wolf had pushed on, following the ascending ridges toward the valley's upper end where more than a foot of new snow lay among the dark spruces that thinned as they straggled upward from the denser stands along the river bottom far below.

As always, the wolves preferred the open slopes, for the wind had scoured them of snow and the frozen shale and angular gravel beneath made travel easy. The black trotted at the head of the pack, followed closely by the gray bitch, the three pups, his adult sons, and finally the resident females. No sound accompanied the wolves, and as they floated along the serpentine ridge crest, the vapor plumes of their breathing were quickly scattered by the gusting wind.

Later, and still higher above the narrowing valley, the big male slowed his pace and dropped over the edge to begin the long slanting descent toward the riverbed. Here the land was badly broken and slashed with almost vertical rock-studded gullies. Dense willow stands and jungles of black-barked alder choked the way, and the pack moved slowly along a common path in the drifting snow.

In its upper reaches, the bed of the Tatlanika had formed in a series of constrictions between steep rocky slopes that defined its sources. Once formed, the main channel had widened and its gradient decreased as it reached the lower valley. It was here that willows began to grow along the ex-posed gravel bars, which widened noticeably as the river spread itself over the more level terrain. Then, still farther downstream, the channels became bordered by runty spruce, the advanced guard of those that had migrated up-ward from the flats and managed to survive. From these gnarled, pitch-saturated trees had come, more than sixty years earlier, the handsawn timbers and boards for the now abandoned placer mine.

The mine was one of several that still occupied the drain-ages of other creeks in the area, and the remnants of three buildings stood on a broad field of gravel adjacent to the river. They shared the slow but undeniable process of decay as they returned to the land. Several derelict sluice boxes stood canted by the high waters of past spring seasons among man-made gravel piles. The troughlike structures had once carried tons of gravel-laden water over their ribbed and burlapped bottoms to collect the final sludge and its flecks of sparse yellow gold. Now the sluices, like the roofless cabin floors, were snow-covered, and only the sag-ging walls of the buildings gave the place definition.

The process of deterioration had been slow in the dryness of the mountains, and during the cold of each seemingly endless winter it was arrested almost completely. Even so, the ancient wood of the structures had long ago turned punky while the steel rods, nuts, bolts, and other hardware that still fastened them together bore caked rust that stained the rough-sawn boards which jutted above the snow. Beneath the slatted floorboards of the buildings, mice, voles, and minuscule shrews lived out brief lives, their presence helping to assure the food supply that the red fox sought with dainty patience.

The vixen was alone now with the onset of winter. She had whelped and reared only two kits during the summer past, and though her pelt had been tufted and sparse at the time of their birth, the youngsters bore little resemblance to their mother. They were dull gray and had grown from four-ounce whelps to subadulthood rapidly, the process governed almost in its entirety by basic instincts established even before their birth. Then, as summer died, they had left the vixen to go their separate ways, and she was alone once more.

Two separate entrance tunnels converged six feet underground to form the main passageway to the den. Dug by the vixen, and others before her, the network consisted of enlargements in a complex of parka-squirrel burrows that veined the talus-saturated hillside above the placer mine. The den contained a partially grass-lined pocket set almost twenty feet beneath the deepest frost line, and in it the vixen would spend at least some of the coldest days during the winter.

Though a bitter wind gusted along the Tatlanika bottoms and blew fluffy snow from the spruces, the early morning sky was clear of clouds. The fox had elected to nap in the slow-growing warmth of a sunny spot that flooded a small, brush-choked clearing among the trees and high up along the valley wall. Here, sheltered by its grass-matted dead branches, she curled tightly on the snow-free trunk of a blow-down spruce, her thick, white-tipped tail lightly covering her pointed muzzle. The rusty redness of her coat blended well with the coarse bark of the tree as she dozed, her dainty jet-black legs tucked beneath her body.

The river-bottom snow was laced with the vixen's delicate track chains. Perfectly spaced lines of the small, round footprints stretched from brush clump to rock, crisscrossed the riverbed itself, and webbed the open hillsides. The black wolf sniffed them with only mild interest before lapping water from the icy trickle beneath the snowcapped stones. The pack had arrived at the placer camp just as the false dawn had begun to dissipate, and the wolves had immediately dispersed to investigate separate parts of the clearing. The black and his adult sons had then circled the largest building, urinating on the stained corner boards before digging randomly in the snow along its foundation.

Many days had passed since the pack had eaten well, and the added burden of the long journey during the previous night had cramped their bellies, making deep sleep impossible. The gray bitch, as was her habit, was the first to select a bed in the granular snow against the boards of the nearest cabin, where she dug a shallow depression in which she circled several times before lying down. The black wolf and his grown sons selected similar places nearby along the sunny side of a sluice frame, while the females curled up close to one another on the open snow near the creek. Then, and only after a final excursion through the doorless cabin shells, the three pups bedded near the old bitch.

Several ravens followed each other as they swooped and glided down the Tatlanika drainage. They paused only long enough to circle over the napping wolves before moving on, still visiting among themselves. The old bitch watched them out of sight before closing her eyes once more, content to enjoy what remained of the sun as its tepid fingers penetrated the long fur over her shoulders and warmed her gray muzzle.

CHAPTER 14

The moose that the old man had selected for his winter's meat was a two-year-old bull and weighed eight hundred pounds. Earlier in the autumn just past, he had tried to consummate his first-time appetite for sex, and in mute testimony to the strength of his adolescent desire bore a slow-healing diagonal slash in the velvety softness of his pendulous snout. His lack of success during the first season of his sexual maturity had come mostly as a result of inexperience and the ludicrous ten-inch palms that he carried on his massive head. They were his first antlers of any substance, having been preceded by almost invisible buttonlike knobs during his first autumn of life.

The weeks between mid-September and late October had seen the young bull driven off repeatedly by older patriarchs as he attempted to share the transient company of the cows they had patiently assembled. The final abortive encounter had been a brief affair as his juvenile grunts reached the ears of a six-year-old bull who outweighed him by more than six hundred pounds. The large animal had met his somewhat hesitant competitor on an open hillside above a willow draw which obscured all but the tantalizing scent of the six cows that had assembled to share his jealous attention. Past failures and the lingering pain of bruised ribs had made retreat easy for the two-year-old as he trotted quickly to make his escape, but not before the big bull's first rush opened the fatty flesh of his muzzle. The raking ivory-tipped palms that spanned more than five feet had been propelled by massive, rut-swollen neck muscles, and the fight was over before it had started.

The biological frustrations of his first breeding year were short-lived, however, diminishing of their own accord as the rut ended during early November. Snowflakes had fallen silently beneath overcast skies as the young bull moved higher among the draws and brush-choked gullies above the place where the Tatlanika River met the Tanana Flats. By the time he entered the Tatlanika's valley, he had grown content with his seemingly hard-fought solidarity.

Then, with retirement, his appetite returned, and he browsed steadily among the dense willow stands in the broad riverbed. Because he had not spent himself in the rut, he retained most of the two-inch layer of hard white fat that overlaid his rump and back, and his post-rut eating added quickly to his already excellent physical condition.

The young bull had selected a stretch of river bottom less than a half mile below Tatum's cabin by mere chance, for it was little different than any other in the wide valley. Here the braided channels formed gravel islands which supported the willows he would need during the long winter ahead. Nearby were spruce groves where the riverbed gave way to slightly higher ground, places where he could lay up during the short daylight hours and, by chewing his cud, digest the prodigious rewards of his feeding.

With the deepening snow, the riverbed had become criss-crossed with the bull's trails and littered with his droppings. His increasingly sedentary existence had gone undisturbed even by the occasional low circlings of the tiny red airplane, an occurrence that had ceased with the first heavy snow. The bull did not fear the plane any more than he feared anything else in his limited surroundings, for he was young and man was unknown to his experience.

The bull represented a potential source from which the herd that was scattered over the foothills and flats below would draw upon for its sustenance in years to come. Prime health, assured by adequate food during the winter ahead, would guarantee the rapid growth of antlers that by next summer would exceed the ones he wore now by more than three times. The immature palms would be shed during midwinter, released from their bases in his skull by the hormone-induced flow of new blood in the tissues that had caused them to grow initially. The sockets left behind by the shed antlers would, for a time, be sensitive and sore, until new skin formed as a prelude to development of the new set.

During the early autumn of his third year, and preparatory for his second rut, his body would fill out, increasing his weight considerably. These changes, along with the zeal of added maturity, would make for a breeding season which would be diametrically different from his first, and success would culminate with pregnancy in a large number of cows.

The huge bull that had forced the two-year-old's retreat into the valley of the Tatlanika no longer existed as the snows of November deepened. Only his antler-stripped skull and hoofed lower legs lay beneath the drifts that obscured most of the frozen gut pile where it was left behind by the hunter who had killed him and driven off his female companions. His carcass had been quickly loaded into the confines of a light airplane, and two flights had been required to finish the task of removing it. In the silence left behind, ravens, black-masked Canada jays, and a gaudy long-tailed magpie had clustered to take their share of the spoils, as did the foxes. Then the snow had come.

Functionally, nothing would change with the absence of the older bull on the breeding meadows during the coming autumn, for he would be replaced by the youngster he had driven off shortly before his demise. The young bull's sperm would be available in greater and more vigorous quantity than would have been possible for the six-year-old, and the older bull's replacement would be proven in coming years by a greater number of healthy calves. For now, however, the young bull was content to indulge himself in solitude, nipping the fibrous willows, and leaving his kidney-shaped beds pressed in the hillside snow above the river.

Both of the gray bitch's male pups now weighed almost eighty pounds, and except for his greater size, a bulk they would never attain, were replicas of their huge sire. Like their smaller, light-gray sister, who at sixty-five pounds would increase her own body size little more, they still lacked the ability to contribute to the over-all well-being of the pack. Despite their adult appearance, and except for the catching of small prey, none of the pups had taken part in the killings. The need to do so would be emphasized during the coming winter but not satisfied as they would continue to rely almost totally upon the adult pack members. No longer would the variety of warmer times be available, and with its disappearance the need for killing prey of greater size on fewer occasions would escalate dramatically. Such killing would depend upon co-operation of the kind possible only in a complex society working in unison toward a common goal. For the nine members of the St. George Creek pack, that goal would be simple survival.

A circling raven cast its flickering shadow among the light spots that still dappled the small clearing, despite the lowering afternoon sun. This, combined with the chill of returning night, roused the vixen from her sleep on the spruce trunk, and she arched her back while stretching her black-stockinged forelegs. Hopping down from her perch, she defecated and emptied her bladder, the act saturating the snow-free space near the dead spruce with her heavy musk. Then, returning to the dryness of the deadfall, she preened her dense, white-tipped tail before slipping away into the grayness of shadow beneath the trees on a course that would take her to the abandoned placer camp near her den.

With darkness at hand, the pack gathered around the black male, and amid the posturing and tail wagging of the others, he stood stiff-legged before once more raising his hind leg against the ancient sluice box. It was the gray bitch, however, who initiated the pack's departure from the placer camp as she trotted to the edge of the flowing water and continued downstream toward the gravel bar that held the snow-buried ruts left by the big tires on Jake Tatum's plane.

CHAPTER 15

Even in the presence of the deepening snow, the open riverbed offered a pathway of least resistance. The fluffy blanket that hid all but the snaking trickle of icy water was only about a foot deep and offered little obstacle to the long-legged wolves as they trotted silently through the darkness that followed a blood-red dusk.

While traveling, wolves are hunting. The truism holds regardless of the time of year, and the need to do so stems less from each participant's immediate hunger than from instinctive habit. Opportunists, as are all wild creatures, wolves possess the added advantage of superior learning ability blended inseparably with a highly co-operative life-style. These factors were at work as the big pack leader negotiated a jumble of bleached and eroded logs which jammed the creek. Beyond this point, the Tatlanika began to narrow as it passed through the lowermost and final constriction of its upper valley.

As if born behind the silent walls of spruce, pastel streamers of bland light undulated like curtains shifting lazily in the wind as the aurora grew with the deepening night. Behind their muted brilliance, which flowed and ebbed rhythmically, stars winked brightly above the silent riverbed. A low moon was already producing vague shadows which latticed the river snow with diagonal patterns, and the wolves were momentarily illuminated as each ghosted across the light shafts between them. The gray bitch followed her mate closely, while the others fanned out when the riverbed allowed for it.

Behind the hunting wolves, their track chains cut the crisscrossed lines left by snowshoe hares where they too crossed the open snow, reluctant to spend more time than was necessary away from the relative protection afforded by the big spruces. On the riverbed, even in the absence of bright moonlight, they sensed their terrible vulnerability to the attacks of the big horned owls, attacks made silent by the downy margins on the birds' flight feathers.

The wolves investigated only the freshest of the tracks, occasionally following them to their termination among the hanging roots and snow-covered logs which bordered the river but seldom going farther into the brush-choked shadows above the high cutbanks.

There are few predators that harbor no interest in the long-eared hares that live out their brief lives among the willow thickets and spruce forests of interior Alaska. Most, however, do not rely exclusively upon the cyclic changes in number that mysteriously produce populations so great that the gullies, swamps, and river bottoms become literally alive with them. The phenomenon requires about ten years to reach its maximum peak, after which the hares disappear almost completely. With their disappearance, the stands of willow upon which they fed stand clipped and girdled to a height which exactly defines the depth of the snow during the preceding winter, and the hares' countless abandoned runways are littered with old desiccated droppings.

Only the tuft-eared lynx relies almost exclusively upon such cyclic plentitude for his own numbers. When the hares exist in great numbers so do the lynx. The big cats' winter dependence upon them is made profitable by instinct-dictated hunting habits and practicable by special anatomical features. Huge powder-puff feet coupled with the cat's relatively light body weight which is exaggerated by his fluffy mottled fur, provide the means by which the cats negotiate deep snow in the same manner as their prey. The claws complement teeth specially developed for holding and tearing. These virtues, coupled with their natural feline swiftness and grace, make the lynx capable of harvesting the snowshoe hare as a staple food while his reliance upon them makes him almost totally dependent upon the hares for his own survival.

The curved line of round, perfectly spaced tracks that regularly touched the edge of the riverbed before continuing downstream held little interest for the wolves. The big tom lynx had followed the river several days before, but in the cold dry air, his smoky scent had quickly vanished. The black wolf visually followed the line of his tracks where they paralleled the riverbank, but only because they followed the direction of his own travel.

As midnight passed, the aurora faded ahead of a full moon, which flooded the Tatlanika bottoms with soft yellow light, and the pack broke out onto the flatness of snow-blanketed gravel near the cabin. All but the gray bitch's pups had been here before and, as always, the big black felt a strange attraction to the squat log building that he knew stood in the darkness beneath the trees ahead.

The building's scent lay heavy over the snow in the opening along the river, and it would be easy to assume that the wolves enjoyed or were attracted to the smell of ancient cooking and the fragrant smokiness of dried pelts. Such scents were, however, only a part of the whole, and were masked by those of the building's occupant. That such scents seemed to attract rather than repel must remain an unsolved paradox, and only the gray bitch held back as the black led the others toward the dark and silent cabin.

Beneath the overhanging roof, and in deep shadow, the snowmobile was formless beneath its battered tarp. Drifting snow had covered most of its bulk, but the black found it easily as he circled the building. Then, after raising his hind leg over a canvas corner that curled from beneath the soft snow, he began to dig.

Moonlight dappled the gray bitch's back as she too circled the building reluctantly, but staying her distance, she moved well back beneath the spruces. Her reluctance stemmed from a thread of fear that curiosity could not overcome, and an hour slipped by before she returned and edged closer to the others as they gathered around the now exposed snowmobile.

The two resident females were absent from the pack, having continued a short distance downriver, and, with wagging tails, the pups easily tore great pieces of the rotting tarp and chased each other for possession of them.

The black, placing his massive paws on the padded seat of the machine, began to lick its vinyl coldness. Then, joined by one of his adult sons, he began methodically to demolish the cold-stiff cushion, scattering bits of yellow plastic and foam rubber on the packed snow. The pair's interest in the man-made objects passed as quickly as it had come, and less than an hour later, under a new dawn, the wolves moved on, resuming their downriver course in the riverbed.

The vixen had discovered the wolves long before her brief stopover at her den, for their scent had reached her nose even as she descended the steep hillside above the now abandoned placer clearing. Finally, stepping out onto the open snow along the river's far bank, she continued to study the open expanses between the abandoned buildings and beyond. Apparently satisfied that she was alone, she trotted cautiously along the perimeter of the clearing, eventually climbing the slope to the den. There, after a brief excursion below ground, she squatted to urinate near the tunnel's mouth before retracing her route to the creekbed, where, like the black wolf, she began to sort through the maze of tracks that led downriver.

After feeding throughout the night, the bull had bedded before first light diluted the total darkness left by the vanishing moon. He had eaten well, and the first and largest of his four stomach chambers was packed with the undigested willow cuttings he had patiently cropped during the hours of darkness. The flat willow island upon which he had selected a bed was a small one, less than a hundred yards long and only half as wide.

Despite the cold, which had deepened noticeably during the night, he was warm. The heavy coat of long, hollow hairs that covered his belly and sides insulated him from the snow, and the heat generated by his massive body quickly melted it, causing it to pack down beneath him. Comfort caused him to doze, even while he coughed up a bolus of twigs and fiber, and his yellow teeth popped softly as his lower jaw rotated slowly with his chewing.

Screened from view by the dense stand of seven-foot willow whips, the bull paid little attention to the coming dawn. A cold wind had begun to gust along the Tatlanika, hissing as it passed through the bankside spruces to spend itself quietly while tumbling gouts of new powder snow from the densely needled boughs. The moose's great ears swung by reflex to test and sift through the small sounds the wind carried. The dry creaking of a dead aspen as it rubbed its neighbor, further polishing the long-healed scar along its trunk, the belling of a raven farther up the drainage that fell and rose on the changing wind, and the soughing of the gusts themselves were all sounds that merely defined the contentment he enjoyed, and he ignored them.

After leaving the cabin, the black wolf and each of his adult sons had killed snowshoe hares during the pack's slow descent of the gently falling riverbed. They had missed several, and had then, on one occasion, spent considerable time among the spruce groves near the river in a futile attempt to interpret the baffling network of scent left by others in the runways that webbed the shadows. Those that had been caught had simply dallied too long on the open snow of the river ahead of the approaching wolves, and had then been too slow to negotiate the cutbank where it ended. They had been swallowed quickly, along with white hair, bones, and viscera, and had not been shared with the others.

The new scent that lingered in the nine intermingled track chains which snaked ahead of the vixen was a measure of the closing distance which separated her from the wolves. As the smell's potency grew, she began to stop more often and peer ahead toward the river's next bend. She had not yet seen the wolves, but she feared their tracks, even as she was drawn to them, just as the black ravens were drawn to such signs, perhaps because of their association with the leavings to be found when those who made them fed.

In the wind-filled lemon light of early morning, the vixen panted rapidly, her dense plumed tail held low as she trotted a zigzag course, further interlacing her own dainty line of footprints with those of the moving wolves ahead. During the night she had stopped to mouse among the deadfalls and brushy thickets above the riverbanks, and had been mildly successful. She had also discovered the blood smears and wisps of downy hair where the wolves had eaten the rabbits they had caught, and the raw scent made her whine thinly. At the third such place, she sat lightly on the snow and barked.

The high-pitched yapping of the fox carried easily on the cold air that washed down the drainage, and the black wolf stopped in mid-stride to listen. As he did, the rest of the pack milled around him, and one of the dun pups whined impatiently before pointing his muzzle into the gusting wind to howl.

The pup's voice was shrill, and the sound surprised him. As a result, he stopped quickly even as it built in volume. As if by a signal, the others milled, their drooping tails wagging earnestly, and the buff males gave voice simultaneously. They were soon followed by the leader, whose deep call rolled among the bends of the river. The pack members were soon touching noses and romping as the gray bitch became the last to howl. The chorus had lasted half a minute, and had stopped abruptly even as it reached the distant slopes that hemmed the valley of the Tatlanika.

For wolves to howl is, quite simply, to communicate. The insistent yapping of the fox had merely been the sound that triggered the pack's desire to do so. For the pup, the vixen's barking probably held some vague instinctive meaning rooted in the eons of time that had made his own existence possible. For him and for the rest as well, the sounds that could be produced at such times were probably a statement of possession that served much the same purpose as did the countless scent posts that the wolves doused with their urine as they traveled over the more than three hundred and fifty square mile area that constituted the territory of the St. George Creek pack. Even though the unseen fox was obviously not a wolf, its voice may have registered as an intrusion of sound, a mild threat to the accepted boundaries of that vast territory, and so the pack howled.

It would have been impossible for the bull to miss the sounds made by the wolves, for he lay less than a half mile downwind to the pack. He had listened to such sounds many times during his brief life, along with·the yammerings of foxes, and they were of no more importance to him than other sounds that were interwoven in the fabric of mundane experience. Even the volume which bespoke their nearness elicited only a slow turn of his massive head and the raising of one fur-lined ear, and because of the brief duration of their howls the bull soon resumed the ceaseless chewing of his cud. Certainly such sounds carried no warning of danger, for the bull had, through the sheerest of coincidence, never encountered those who made them. Even had he possessed a more intimate knowledge of the gray forms that older moose grow accustomed to, the howling would have represented no danger to his well-being, for wolves do not howl before, during, or after a kill.

Because of the gusts that blew from behind them and ruffled the long hairs of their backs, the wolves had, as yet, not discovered the bull with their noses. They continued in their descent of the river to a point less than a quarter mile from him before they found his still-fresh tracks. Nuzzling the fresh deep-cut hoofprints, the black worked his way into a small stand of willow, followed closely by his adult sons and the three pups. The others fanned out, each seeking his or her own scent source, and a horned owl glided unseen and unheard from a roosting place in a tall bankside spruce after watching the pack from a distance. No single track set defined the direction in which the bull lay, yet the tangled network served as a powerful indicator, for its potency increased tangibly as the wolves followed it haltingly downstream.

The dubious advantage of first discovery was held by the moose, and he spotted the wolves as they came into view from behind the river's bend immediately above the island upon which he lay. His cavernous nostrils had told him of the pack's coming long before, and as he watched the gray bitch, his chewing stopped. Then he turned his head away as if doing so would better define what his eyes had seen.

It was the gray bitch who discovered the bull. Because he had bedded for a short time among the spruce a few hundred yards upstream before selecting the willow island, the black had worked patiently to find the pool of scent that still lingered in the snow-packed depression left by his body. All but the gray bitch had joined him in his quest, and as she advanced across the open snow on the river, her eyes caught the movement of the bull's ears above the short, leafless willows.

The old wolf trotted boldly toward the moose, and as she drew near, he grunted mildly with the effort required to stand and face her.

After a cursory investigation of the moose's temporary bed in the deep powder snow, the black and the others returned to the riverbed. Moments later they rounded the bend to join the gray bitch and, as one, spotted him where he now loomed blackly above the willow tops. They quickly formed a half circle around him, the leader and his sons downwind, where they could now feel the blanket of warmth that flooded their noses. Only the small noises made by the wind disturbed the silence.

His lack of past experience with wolves was the only factor that prevented the bull from bolting. The nearness of the pack did, however, cause the first fluttering of instinctive fear, but it was masked by a mild belligerence, probably rooted in the sudden invasion of his small private world by intruders he could not identify. As a result, the long hairs along his muscular neck rose uncertainly while his big ears flattened themselves beneath the bases of his small antlers.

Patience, even among wild creatures, is a learned habit formed only through constant repetition, and it represented the one reaction on the part of the bull that would have forestalled the inevitable. Had it been present in greater quantity, it might even have prevented indefinitely the events which followed. But, because the bull was still too young to exercise such control over his normal inclination to flee, he swung toward the open side of the half circle made by the wolves, his hooves slewing in the soft dryness of loose gravel beneath the snow as he started to trot toward the open river channel adjacent to the willow island.

Even as the bull took his first step, the black wolf, his

mate, and their adult sons were on their feet and closing upon the broad rump that rippled with the surging of the bull's powerful hind legs. His spontaneous bid for escape was not made in blind panic, yet it provided the single most critical necessity for the triggering of the wolves' attack. If at that moment panic had been a factor, the black and his mate would have sensed it, and their first lunge would have been made with less caution.

With his tail held low, less than three long bounds were required by the black wolf to close the gap, and in a blur of movement, he launched his body over the bull's pumping hind hooves. Collision and the action of the black's two-inch canine teeth occurred at exactly the same instant, and though the big wolf's intent was to grasp and hold, his teeth merely tore long rents in the contracting muscle strands beneath the tight rump skin and ludicrously small stub of the moose's tail. Then the black's feet struck the snow once more, and he rolled before veering away.

Pain coursed instantly down the bull's hocks and up over his great hindquarters, causing him to grunt audibly and blow great clouds of vapor into the cold air. He would have stopped to face the small, musky animals that plagued him and provided the only physical pain he had ever felt beyond that inflicted by the big bull in the autumn just past had the attack of one of the buff males not followed closely upon that of the black.

The tan wolf's charge enabled him to obtain a deep hold along the inner surface of the bull's right ham. The pain elicited by his jaws was somewhat neutralized by that produced already by the pack leader, but it provided the last bit of impetus needed to unleash the blind panic that caused the bull to slip and almost fall as he erupted from the willows of the island and out onto the openness of the riverbar. As he did so, the gray bitch made her own bid for part of the kill.

Slipping beneath the bull's heaving belly, the old female somehow managed to avoid his front hooves and secure a loose hold in the throat skin just below the swinging bell. She was then dragged along, her legs flailing in a futile attempt to recontact the soft snow. Moments later she felt the icy water as the bull reached the open channel and, without pause, lunged into the river current. He finally stopped to kick viciously and, in doing so, dislodged the buff wolf that rode his rump.

The gray bitch's teeth being age-worn caused her grip on the bull's throat to fail soon after she obtained it, and a violent shake of his massive antlered head tossed her heavily into the cold river.

Bright scarlet coursed downward over the gray smoothness of the bull's inner thighs before spending itself in the black water that sucked at his legs. The pain that flowed from the torn muscles of his rump had ebbed slowly to be replaced by shock, and as a result he was unaware of the open rent in the skin and flesh of his lower neck.

Just as his flight had been a signal to attack, his abrupt stop quickly became the catalyst which provided relief from it. The wolves retreated and regrouped on the open snow of the island a few yards from the water's edge. Tongues lolled with exertion, and the gray bitch's pups advanced eagerly to lap at the congealing patches of redness in the snow, which ended where the bull's tracks entered the water. The others, those who had entered the fray, panted audibly in the still air, the plumes of their warm breath layering among them as they lay and sat upon the snow. After the passage of long minutes, the black stood and once more trotted boldly toward the head-hung bull.

Following the big wolf's lead, his sons also approached the water's edge, but quickly swung downstream in doing so. From this position, they suddenly broke into a loping run, bounding across a shallow riffle. The movement caused the bull to swing his head as he watched the pair make their bid for a position behind him. Then he bolted once more toward a narrow finger of gravel that still separated him from the spruces which bordered the river.

The black watched his sons as they slowed where the current deepened at mid-channel. As they regained solid footing and cut diagonally toward the point at which the bull would emerge from the river, the black also leaped into the current to follow.

Running low to the ground, and unhampered now by the current, the first of the buff males met the bull as he trotted onto the gravel spit. The moose's heaving sides and labored breathing attested to his growing exhaustion, which was aggravated by shock and insidious panic. As a result, it was easier this time to pause just beyond the water's edge as he met the tan wolf's charge. The bull's sudden stop caused the buff wolf to miss the hold he sought under the bull's neck, and his snapping jaws closed on nothing more than cold air. Skidding in the snow, he switched ends and this time his leap was face-on to the bull, and successful.

Once more jagged waves of blinding pain swept upward as long teeth locked in the rubbery softness of the bull's muzzle. Nowhere in his vast body were there more sensitive pain centers than here, and the buff wolf's grip acted as a ring in the nose of an intractable farmyard bull. The weight of his attacker was more than enough to hold the bull's head down, and the two animals faced each other in a grim tug-of-war.

Braced on his spread forelegs, the bull defecated freely while turning slowly, still held fast by the buff male. As he did, he felt rather than saw the attack of the second male, once more high on his blood-slippery hindquarters. As the wolf struck him, panic once more became boundless and the bull began swinging his head from side to side in an agonized attempt to dislodge the wolf that held his nose. Simple preoccupation with the pain inflicted by his own efforts and the scent-rich nearness of the animal that held his nose made him oblivious to all else, and he was unaware of the fact that his belly, just ahead of his right hind leg, had already been opened by the black. It was at this instant that the buff wolf's grip on the bull's nose failed, as the septum which divided the flared nostrils tore.

Had the tan wolf's grip released earlier or later than the moment it did, he would have been thrown clear of the bull's hooves by simple momentum. As it was, he dropped between them, and before he could scramble clear, he was pinned to the frozen, unyielding gravel that underlined the snow.

The bull's hoof thrust was not an accident. Backed by more than a half ton of weight and driven by the musculature of his upper foreleg, it quickly crushed the tan wolf's fragile chest, driving the splintered ribs deeply into his heart and lungs. He was dead even before the reflex spasms that flexed his legs dragged his lifeless body into the flowing river, to be carried quickly downstream where it slipped unnoticed by the others beneath a shelf of ice, and vanished.

The torn snow beneath the bull was now laced liberally with his blood, for in addition to exposing a loop of intestine, the black's teeth had torn several of the big, convoluted veins that underlay the thin skin of his abdomen. Continued bleeding and the overwhelming shock that numbed even the stabbing pain in his torn muzzle weakened him further, and he grunted raggedly, blowing a fine mist of red vapor from his mutilated nose.

Sensing its victory, and still unaware that it had lost one of its ranks, the pack rested a mere dozen feet from the swaying bull. Once more, the wolves formed a semicircle, and the gray bitch stretched on her belly in the snow. Like the others, she panted heavily with the exertion of the past minutes, and her long tongue flicked the snow between her front legs.

Midday passed slowly, and sometime during the afternoon, the sun slipped beneath a heavy layer of cloud. With its disappearance, and pushed by a new wind, the air warmed slightly. Several of the ever-present ravens perched quietly among the needle-barren top branches of the nearby spruces, as if content to await the inevitable climax of the drama they had watched unfold on the riverbar below.

Other eyes also watched from the broken hillside above the Tatlanika. The vixen had circled away from the river and found the pack and its kill easily with her nose. For now, she was content to nap among the snow-covered logs and charred stumps that told of an ancient fire that had once swept the hillside. Like the ravens, she too would wait her turn.

CHAPTER 16

The bull died just after full darkness enveloped the Tatlanika River. Blood loss and the massive shock which accompanied it had slowly robbed him of the ability to stand. With death near at hand, his attention span had become dangerously short, making him unable to watch the waiting wolves for more than brief periods. It had been during one such lapse that his front legs had buckled and his great body collapsed slowly onto the snow. Though he vaguely sensed his vulnerability, it had, by then, been far too late, and his attempt to regain his feet resulted only in a dizzying loss of balance which caused him to roll heavily onto his side. The pack had begun to feed immediately, and its members were unaware of the point at which the bull's eight-pound heart pulsated weakly for the last time before ceasing its fibrillation and stopping completely.

The kill, like most made by wolves, had been more the result of fortuitous events than intelligent action on the part of the pack. Contrary to the many legends, the gray wolf relies heavily upon simple good luck in the securing of his livelihood. No complex plan had been devised or executed, and no deliberate method had been employed in the conversion of a half ton of healthy, living moose to nutritious food.

In the killing of the bull, no single wolf had been more or

less important than another, at least among those who actively participated. Even the pair of resident bitches had taken part. Though their quick rushes had produced little damage to the dying bull, they had by harassment served to weaken him further. Though both were more than capable of contributing tangibly to the over-all effort, this had been the first time since joining the group led by the black that they had done so.

The big black wolf was, perhaps, the most effective member of the pack. Wise in the ways of the big moose that he had sought for many years and helped kill in the dozens, he also carried the possible advantage of abnormal body weight. His presence was, therefore, indispensable. Most important, he possessed the vast skill that time had imparted, and he used it to maximum advantage.

The part played by the small gray bitch could be easily underestimated. She weighed no more than the biggest of her three pups, and was an old wolf. Her phenomenal age among those of her kind, though providing a wealth of experience, was, in the end, a factor which limited her physical contribution to the killings. Yet, as was her way, she had taken a familiar though subtle liberty with the casual dominance her mate held over her. She had done this by selecting the route taken by the pack as it left the placer digs on the upper river. It had been the course she had set that had culminated in the discovery of the bull. The choice had not been a conscious one, rather the result of impulsive surrender to the gentle proddings of habit that was itself the result of her long lifespan. Simply stated, the old female instinctively recognized the value of hunting the willows that fringed the river, for she sensed that moose preferred them.

The adult sons of the black and the gray bitch, though subservient to both parents, had added their own special talents to the demise of the two-year-old bull. Their principal worth had been found in their superb strength, for both had been of prime age and in excellent health. The one that had been killed would, during subsequent times, be sorely missed, but for now his death was ignored, principally because the act of feeding seemed to supersede its importance.

Though killing was no longer a new experience for them, the gray bitch's pups were still rank amateurs in the venture. They lacked the finesse, agility, and, more important, the courage that would come only with added maturity. Though they were, to the eye, adults, they also lacked the depth of musculature and the ability to expose it instantly to fatigue in a short, violent burst of total physical endeavor.

Only they failed to make any contribution in the killing of the bull. Their nonparticipation came as a result of simple fear of the animal that faced them. As the attack had begun, they had shied away to once more become anxious bystanders to the drama, which caused them to pant nervously from their position of safety behind the screening willow brush.

Heavy snow fell once more during the week that followed the kill on the Tatlanika. The St. George Creek wolves had gorged on the fresh meat, feeding several times during the first day, and while doing so, a method based upon preference had attended their eating.

Probably because of the mutilated condition of the torn hindquarters and the gouts of severed muscle exposed to them, they had consumed most of that portion first. Then the skin covering the bull's cavernous abdomen had been stripped away along with the long-fibered flesh that covered his flat rib bones. Because the bull was in prime condition, such efforts were rewarded by heavy deposits of lacy white mesenteric fat that festooned the spaces between the internal organs. The wolves consumed it greedily before pulling the ropy intestines onto the packed snow, and by dusk of the second day, even these had vanished.

The bull's twenty-pound liver was eaten next, and because of the quantity of meat they had consumed, and the repetitive nature of their feeding, the scats of the eight wolves were once more loose and dark where they speckled the white snow. If there was waste, it occurred here through the inefficiency of digestive tracts overworked by quantity rather than a failure to consume what they had killed.

Even in the utilization of what is killed, the gray wolf is almost perfectly equipped. The long canine teeth, or fangs, that made the kill reality were now used to grasp and move parts of the moose as the feeding continued. The premolars behind them served in the tearing of smaller chunks from those that were too large to swallow. Such chunks were then swallowed whole.

As the first day slipped by, the impulse to feed excessively quickly passed, and the wolves rested more, always within a short distance of the carcass, which by now bore little re-semblance to its original shape and size. As some of the pack dozed in the weak warmth during the brief days that fol-lowed, other members left the river to hunt on their own. The black and his buff son were, as a result, absent for pe-riods of up to a half day. The pack's stay at the kill was a short one despite the hunger each wolf had brought to the Tatlanika, and as the pack moved on, others moved in to gain their expected share of what remained. Ravens, Can-ada jays, chickadees, several short-tailed weasels, and a soli-tary, orange-throated pine marten fed while the pack dozed or was absent. The marten, a weasel-like tree dweller, was drawn to the carcass more by simple curiosity than were the others, and his feeding was a game as he dodged the rushes of the pups. Boldest of all were the white-collared Canada, or gray, jays, and they often fed wing to shoulder with the wolves, who ignored their presence.

The fastidious vixen had quickly become a regular at the kill. She possessed the uncanny ability to determine when the wolves were well fed, and at such times she advanced cautiously to snap up a small frozen chunk of meat and then retreat quickly with it to the willows that bordered the spruce at the bar's edge. On several occasions, the gray bitch's pups chased her, but such pursuits were a game as they were with the dark-furred marten. Mostly the pups tolerated the fox, as did the rest of the wolves.

The pack resumed its hunting during the fourth night following the kill, and all but the resident females accompanied the black as he left the carcass on a downriver course. Later, under a starless sky, the wolves found a barren cow moose among the snags and willow jungles where the Tatlanika became part of the broad flats. Fifteen miles from the carcass of the bull, the cow was a large one, weighing well over a thousand pounds. High-humped and gaunt, however, she stood her ground while callously ignoring the presence of the pack. Her disdain was well rooted in long experience, for she was older than most, and aided by the dense willows in which she stood. As a result, and after only a brief quarter hour, the black gave up and led the rest away on a line that took the pack back to the Tatlanika. The wolves arrived there shortly after dawn.

With the coming of December, the blanket of snow on the flats lay well over three feet thick on level ground, and far deeper where the sporadic wind gusted and piled it in hard-packed drifts among the stunted spruce that grew on the slopes along the foot of the desolate mountains. The relative warmth of early winter had quietly vanished with the cessation of the snowfall and clearing skies. The clouds that produced the snow had mantled the earth with an insulating blanket, warding off the cold layer of air that rested at higher altitudes. With their disappearance, it grew bitterly cold, and the residual warmth of the land vanished as moisture fell from the inverted air layers in the form of minute ice crystals.

The black had taken the pack onto the flats after staying less than a week on the Tatlanika kill. He had traced a route along the lower river to a point just west of the place where Fish Creek swung away to flow due north toward its obscure junction with the Wood. In the deep snow, the wolves traveled single file, leaving a trough of track sign as they passed. The black and his adult son broke trail on most days, and the pack rested frequently, often covering less than eight miles during the almost twenty-hour nights. During the intermittent brief periods of daylight, they sought out open ponds and sloughs upon which to doze and lick the coarse pads of their feet, which were nicked by shards of ice and unseen branch stubs beneath the heavy snow.

The pack found little to justify its abandonment of the carcass on the Tatlanika. Even the snowshoe hares were less easily caught as they ghosted away, bounding easily on the deep powder snow with their densely furred feet. In the dry cold, ice particles fogged the distant horizon and sparkled dull orange against the low sun. The periods of daylight were now less than four hours long, and during the long nights the cold deepened until it became a tangible entity which shrunk the mercury in the rusty thermometer beneath the eaves of Jake Tatum's far-off cabin to the final mark of its lower scale.

CHAPTER 17

Tatum's return to the cabin on the Tatlanika was un-
obtrusive. It was also late. Personal business in Fairbanks
had frustrated his departure and his self-made deadline of
November 15 had been exceeded by almost a full month.
Ice fog had, by then, mantled the city by the Chena River
once more, turning Christmas decorations on lampposts to
lifeless, frost-encased statuary. The old man had thought of
such things as the plane climbed into the clear cold air that
was stained with pastel noonday light, and it had been good
to leave.

After crossing the flats in air so smooth that little was
required beyond pointing the airplane in the proper direction, and then banking into the broad mouth of the lower
Tatlanika Valley, habit and the realization that it would be
his last time aloft for several months had caused the old man
to drop lower over the snow-blanketed riverbed and then
follow it to its head in the foothills. Because of this, he had
caught a brief glimpse of the kill made by the St. George
Creek wolves.

Immediately after spotting the familiar "spoked wheel" of
tracks, he climbed steeply, turning in the tight confines of
the upper valley. As he circled, the sign told him several
things simultaneously. That it was an old kill was apparent

by the absence of wolves and by the soft contours of the
main trails where they radiated outward onto the river before disappearing beneath the dark spruces which bordered
the opposite bank. Other track signs were also present
where foxes had woven their own prints among those left by
the wolves, and, nearer the carcass, he saw the cobweb
specklings of raven tracks. Though it was an imperfect esti-
mate, the old man guessed that the kill had been made by a
small pack, and judging by the accumulation of new snow
over the sign, that it was at least a week old.

Even as seen through the frosted Plexiglas windows of the
moving plane, it was apparent that little remained of the
kill. The old man assumed that it represented the bull he
had watched and planned on for a supply of fresh meat for
himself during the months to come. Then, dropping lower,
the tips of the tall spruces scant feet away from his wing tip,
he had seen the smallish antler palm that protruded above
the snow. With his suspicions confirmed, he had angrily
popped the control stick rearward, making the plane leap
upward above the trees, then pounded his knee with a
balled fist as he continued upriver.

After sliding to a stop in the deep cushion of snow on the
riverbar adjacent to the cabin, he had tailed the airplane
around until it faced away from the willows. After rolling
two cement-filled fuel drums down the gentle bank, he had
turned them on end and tied the plane's wings securely with
ropes to the rings embedded in each.

The old man worked quickly, his anger momentarily forgotten in the finger-numbing pain wrought by the biting
cold. With the airplane secured to the heavy drums, he
paused for breath before dropping to his knees to lash its
tail to a willow clump nearby. As he tied the final knot, he
felt a mild tightness in his chest and had stared unseeing at
the plane's red tail fin while the sensation passed. Then,
after once more blaming the tingling pain and shortness of

breath upon old age and another sedentary summer in town, he completed the chore.

With the aircraft's engine cooling quickly, he then broke a trail to the cabin to retrieve an empty, and topless five-gallon gas tin. The crude hand-made bucket was fitted with a heavy wire bail, and into it he drained the engine's oil. Had he not done this, it would have quickly solidified in the cold to a gelatinous mass, making the draining and a future engine start impossible. The two gallons of syrupy oil would be stored in the cabin, where they could be placed upon the Yukon stove, warmed, and then poured back into the engine when needed.

Leaving the oversized balloon-tired wheels in the plane where he had packed them before leaving town, the old man finished by slipping fitted nylon covers over the wings before carrying the oil and other odds and ends to the silent cabin. The old husky followed on his heels, reluctant to break her own trail through the deep snow and happy to be free of the airplane's cramped and odorous interior.

It seemed much colder inside the cabin than it had outside, as the old man teased a half-filled pressure lantern into reluctant light. Watching as the flimsy mantle sucked at the flame and then glowed with light, he remembered as always an acquaintance who had been horribly burned and disfigured by a full lantern that had exploded after being lit before the white gas in its tank could warm properly and expand. Like whiskey, supercooled gasoline was a danger that few appreciated.

In the hissing lantern's cold light, he found kindling and the rusted stove soon puffed noisily, drawing properly only after the warmth had driven the column of cold air from the tin chimney. As the fire took hold, the stove ticked metallically, its ancient cast-iron door tapping to the tune of draft gusts that sent fragrant smoke whisking across the snow-encased roof and into the nearby trees. As always, these sounds and smells seemed to make the cabin come to life, a sensation that comforted the old man as he rubbed his gnarled hands together over the slowly warming stove top.

The low sun continued along its brief pathway to the horizon, and the shadows in the river valley had deepened quickly. It had been full dark as the old man completed the task of unloading the last of the supplies he had packed in the airplane. Then, after warming his hands once more, he followed the snow-free path beneath the cabin's eaves to the woodpile behind the building. In the patch of light that spilled through the window, he discovered the mutilated snowmobile.

Stooping, he brushed snow from the platform that once supported the machine's foam seat. After returning to the cabin for the lantern, he examined the snow-covered tracks that were still evident nearby, then slipped the heavy moose-hide mitten from his right hand to facilitate picking up several brittle scraps of torn plastic. In the darkness above the lantern's circle of bright light, he swore softly.

Closer in under the cabin's low, overhanging eaves, he studied several still-clear track prints in the powdery earth, and they told the story of the vandalized machine clearly. A single print was huge, and the old man stooped to marvel at the size of the wolf that had made it before retracing his steps to the cabin.

After shoving several pitch-laden spruce splits into the stove and shedding his parka, he poured coffee from the blackened pot before sitting down at the table. Little doubt remained that the same wolves were the cause of his deprivation at the old kill, and his annoyance over the stripped snowmobile seat grew. The bull moose had been his by prior claim, and though there were other moose in the valley, to his knowledge none were as close and therefore as handy to his needs. He had, in fact, spotted several track sets where they crossed the riverbed, but more than five miles below the cabin. To kill a moose that far away, even with the aid of the snowmobile, would represent an arduous task.

As he sipped the coffee, his thoughts returned to the machine. Its ruin seemed to represent an almost calculated act of outright vandalism, and though he had no real proof, its perpetration by the same wolves that had killed the bull magnified his proprietary attitude toward the moose. The old man took these thoughts to bed with him, where he lay listening to the softly collapsing ashes in the dampered stove before sleep claimed him.

The following morning, after reviewing the events that had transpired the night before, his first inclination had been to snowshoe downriver to the kill and "set on it," and he would have probably done so had his traps and other tackle been ready for use. He reasoned that the wolves might return to the remains of the bull at some future time, but he had no way of knowing when. Experience told him that little of the carcass remained beneath its covering of snow except for a few scraps of freeze-hardened hide, perhaps a section of well-picked backbone, and the antlered skull he had seen from aloft. The old man had, during his long life, seen hundreds of wolf kills and each bore the characteristics whose sameness made such prediction possible. As a trapper and airplane hunter, he knew from his fleeting look at the kill site more than just the position at which the carcass rested upon the riverbar.

The cache stood well away from the cabin in its own small clearing among the shadowy trees. Built in the traditional manner with small peeled logs, it was almost an exact duplicate of the bigger building, differing only in size and the twelve-foot poles upon which it was supported. Each of its legs had been wrapped in its own sheath of tin stovepipe to a height of almost four feet as a deterrent against gnawing rodents such as the porcupine and red squirrels. The cache held most of the old man's supplies.

Tins of flour, corn meal, salt, and other dry foods were stacked in its dark interior and would be kept dry by the cache's needle-layered tar-paper roof. Along with the edibles, there were several rusty tins of pearl oil, or kerosene. The pungent oil was no longer used, having been replaced by the more volatile white gas, or Blazo fuel, that the old man burned in the pressure lantern.

Old pieces of tarp and rope, along with an ancient block and tackle set, hung on rusted nails driven deeply into the cache's log walls. A plumber's stove that lay covered by several old tattered blankets of military origin completed the inventory. All was shut away in darkness by a heavy, leather-hinged door, while outside and beneath the structure's floor a cluster of broken traps hung idly in permanent shadow.

Tatum spent the first day on the Tatlanika transferring supplies from the cache to the cabin, and moving the heavy snowmobile inside where it would frost heavily before warming enough to start. Only then did he direct his full attention to his traps.

Fortified with scalding coffee, the old man began by building a roaring fire of dry spruce logs beneath the trees and well away from the cabin. He then settled half of an empty fifty-five-gallon drum over the flames and deepening bed of hot coals. Finally, using an ax, he chopped through the creek ice where the current slowed and formed a deep pool below the cabin. From this he hauled buckets of water and emptied each into the drum. Several trips were required to half fill it; the work was slow, and as he made the final trip to the river he noticed that black water was already welling up through the hole and freezing where it ran out onto the river ice. Kept open, the hole would provide drinking water throughout the winter.

After stoking the fire, the old man went inside, where, once more sitting at the oilcloth-covered table, he noticed that his hands took longer to warm than they had last year. This fact seemed more difficult to accept than his shortness of breath, perhaps because it limited his every move, and sleep came slower that night, despite his weariness.

In the first pale light of late morning, the drum began to boil as the old man hurried it by stacking more logs against its base. To the steaming water he then added two full bags of a substance known to him only as Logwood Crystals. The deep cobalt-colored salts dissolved rapidly, permeating the air with their cloying odor, and steam rose upward to gather as heavy frost on the spruce branches overhead. Then, after threading a steel rod through the rings affixed to the ends of the drag chains on several big traps, he immersed them and laid the rod across the edges of the drum. They were the first of more than a hundred that he would treat in this fashion.

The process of boiling traps was an old one used by most trappers and it served two purposes. First, it removed the light film of oil that was applied to all new traps to keep them from rusting. For the old man, this was an academic benefit, for all of his traps were well used, many of them as old as himself. They had been boiled, however, each year, and herein could be found the second purpose served by the dissolved crystals.

In addition to blackening the traps with a film that retarded rust, the pungent liquid destroyed scent. Ordinary handling and storage during the off-season applied odors to the traps which had to be neutralized before the traps were used. Once treated, the traps would carry no scent except for the faintly resinous, woody odor of the crystals themselves. Handled with clean cotton gloves that had been washed without soap and dried for long weeks in the summer sun, the traps would, when set, provide no clue to their origin.

As he worked, the old man was aware of the rasping

sounds made by the plastic bag in which he kept a supply of
the special cotton gloves. The bag moved with the slight
breeze that blew from the river. Hung in a clump of willow,
it would remain closed and away from the cabin until its
contents were needed.

As Tatum hung the first cluster of big traps to dry in the
cold air, he chatted with the husky, and she responded by
stretching on her front legs and whining deeply. The old
man's traps were much more than a mere collection of useful gadgets. Each had its own unique origin, and several
styles were represented. They were all big traps, numbers
114 and 4½ Newhouses predominating. When set, the jaws
of either would span more than ten inches between powerful double springs that activated them when released by the
sensitive trigger pan in the center. Purchased new, such
traps bore a staggering price tag, costing more than $90
each. The old man estimated his own investment at well
over $5,000.

Tatum had altered the number 114s to suit his own needs
by removing the wicked, factory-installed spiked teeth each
jaw was equipped with, and he had often chuckled
mirthlessly over the regulation that made such traps illegal a
few years earlier. The model was, as a result, no longer man-
ufactured, the company that made it having been pressured
by environmental groups who had reasoned that such teeth
were inhumane. Long before the law had been passed, the
old man had decided that the teeth were a disadvantage
rather than a benefit where holding a caught animal was
concerned. They shattered leg bones, he had reasoned, tearing the flesh of a wolf's leg, thus providing less bearing and
holding power. Others had scoffed, but Tatum was stub-
bornly convinced that the alteration was worthwhile.

To the old man and most other wolfers, inhumanity was
not a consideration in the business of trapping. Therefore,
the changes wrought by those he considered to be over-

zealous outsiders were nothing more than annoyances. With passage of the new law banning the toothed Newhouse trap, he had found private amusement, assuming that those he hated had inadvertently played into his hands.

The modifications that the old man carefully made to his traps extended well beyond their jaws. By doubling the length of the drag chains with which each trap was equipped and skillfully welding the splice, he had discovered that fewer animals escaped. In addition, the longer chains made the hooked steel drags more effective and less likely to pull loose once caught.

Just as the old man scoffed at those who coated their traps with hot wax to lubricate and destroy scent, he also disdained the use of freshly cut logs as drags. The steel drags he used resembled huge, double-armed fishhooks more than sixteen inches long, their free ends twisted cleverly so that the devices tumbled along their central axis when pulled by a leg-caught animal. The sharp hooks easily penetrated the snow rather than sliding over its surface as a log would, and grabbed securely any object that fell in their paths.

Much later, the spring traps boiled and hung on spikes in nearby trees, the old man turned his attention to the more than ten dozen snares. Made of braided, high-tensile steel the thickness of an ordinary drinking straw, each was more than seven feet in length. Lasso-like, the closing end bore a device of marvelous simplicity yet deadly effectiveness. The old man and most other trappers knew the name Raymond Thompson well, and the ingenious device he had invented.

Composed of a small rectangle of bent steel which assumed the shape of a shallow Z, the lock bore two holes, one in each of its ends. Through one, the end of the cable was attached permanently by a compressed steel sleeve, while through the other, the same cable slid freely, making a simple noose. When sliding closed, the lock moved freely, but because of its shape would not loosen when pressure was applied in the reverse direction, and the noose only tightened more as its victim struggled.

Until the Canadian trapper's invention became a reality, trappers contented themselves with simple wire nooses. They had been poor substitutes for the locked snare, however, and more animals escaped than were caught. Because of this, early trappers were severely handicapped and developed an almost total reliance upon the more cumbersome steel spring traps for the taking of wolves and other big fur bearers.

The old man recognized the failings of the big Newhouses. They were certainly more difficult to conceal, much heavier to pack along a trapline, and often rendered harmless by the thawing and refreezing of the snow that concealed them. Finally, they were expensive, making the collections used by serious trappers worth many thousands of dollars, an investment which limited the number of men who practiced the trapping of wolves to the exclusion of other fur bearers.

The neatly coiled snares took little time to boil, and the old man stamped his feet on the packed snow as the flames beneath the boiling drum receded. In the darkness, the deep bed of red coals shimmered with glowing heat, and seemed to float disembodied before the old man's tired eyes. Then, removing the final clusters of blackened snares from the steaming liquid and hanging them with the others, he walked the short distance to the cabin, and the husky whine-yawned behind him before curling up in the deep shadows along the cabin.

The old trapper's eyes burned with fatigue and the irritating fumes of the logwood vapor as he idly watched the congealing bacon grease on his plate and sipped the river water and whiskey that half filled the chipped enamel cup. It had not occurred to him to question the urgency with which he had worked throughout the day, but had he done so, the kill downriver would have amply justified it. It begged to be set, and come morning it would be, but for now he satisfied himself once more with the imaginary placement of the snares he had decided to use. The remains of the bull's carcass were not ideally situated for his plan, but long years of experience would compensate.

Later, the cabin's interior plunged into total darkness except for the shafts of dancing orange light that passed through the vent slits in the stove's door, the old man listened to the muted calling of an owl somewhere beyond the silent river. Then the bunk springs creaked as he rolled over to face the log wall, and his mind's picture of the kill blurred in sleep.

CHAPTER 18

December's third week terminated in the winter solstice, and with it came the dark season's shortest days. Barely three hours of half-daylight followed a prolonged dawn, which then faded quickly in a premature twilight, and did nothing to ease the deep cold that gripped the valley of the Tatlanika River and the vast flats beyond. The frozen land lay silent and untouched by wind as the spruces became unmoving spires of hanging, rime frost-encased snow. The cold, even in its prolonged severity, failed to close the deeper stronger-flowing creeks completely, and many of them, like the upper Tatlanika, still showed open water in a few places. Where the flow still prevailed, dense clouds of white vapor formed where the air contacted the warmer water and plumed upward to layer the naked willows with sparkling ice crystals.

After leaving the valley, the black wolf had pushed a trail eastward, and the pack once more broke out onto the flatness of the Wood River ice at high noon. Backed by weak lemon-tinted light, their legs cast grotesque moving shadows outward on the even whiteness and their panting plumed densely, its vapor assuming the color of the low sun.

Having reached the open riverbed, the pack closed upon the big leader and milled about him with wagging tails.

Perhaps it had been the cramping numbness produced by an almost total absence of food or simply the bitter cold that had pushed the big wolf to extend the pack's nighttime travel well into the short hours of light. Whatever the reason, upon reaching the Wood the new urgency was apparent, and he paused only long enough to choose a downriver course before breaking into the ground-eating trot that had been denied him in the deep snow. In less than an hour, another night would begin.

Two days earlier it had looked as if the pack's luck in hunting had been restored. While crossing the largest of several shadow-laced clearings, each containing a frozen pond, the wolves had blundered upon a large bull moose. An immediate rush had been made but it failed once more in its primary purpose of causing the animal to turn and flee.

After more than an hour of waiting punctuated by short ineffective attacks, the wolves moved off, despite their hunger-shrunken bellies. No blood had been drawn, and after only a short wait, the bull had walked slowly into the elongating shadows cast by the dense trees that circled the opening and began to browse stoically among the short willows.

With the gathering darkness, the silence that lay over the flats seemed to deepen. It was as if the cold had produced a vacuum which sucked even the smallest of sounds from the frozen air. Along the course of the meandering Wood River, the ever-present jays were apparently content to sit among the dark, secret places provided by dense spruce branches, their feathers fluffed to insulate them from the bitter cold.

A half-moon rode low in the black band of sky beyond the Wood River, faintly illuminating the unbroken snow ahead of the black wolf. As the pack fanned out behind him, he scooped snow with his mouth at frequent intervals while scarcely breaking the rhythmic trotting gait which he and the others assumed as they traveled on the open riverbed.

The powder snow partially slaked the wolves' thirst, but only with the consumption of large quantities, and the process was a tedious one at best. As a result, the black stopped at the first open water he found, and the pack lapped noisily in the black water that slipped silently beneath a small opening in the ice.

Their thirst satisfied, the gray bitch and resident females investigated the flat, grooved trail of an otter that stretched from the drinking place to the riverbank, but it was old and bore no scent.

Several miles ahead of the wolves two moose were bedded in the snow adjacent to the riverbank. During the weeks just past, the cow and her calf had experienced little real difficulty in negotiating the deep snow which had long before buried the bases of the willow shoots among which they fed. For them, food had been plentiful enough, and they had browsed leisurely throughout the cold nights.

The calf weighed almost seven hundred pounds now, considerably more than he had on that peaceful evening in autumn when he had first met the St. George Creek pack. Like the big cow, however, he had forgotten the warmer season just as he had forgotten the wolves.

The cow was pregnant once more, her rut quest having been a successful venture, and a single fetus floated in the vast wet warmth of her massive belly. Nourished by the fibrous willow and sealed away from the subzero cold, it would replace the big calf that stood by her side. For now, however, both needed a mother, each in its own way.

The almost patternless wanderings of the two moose had started with the deepening snow and at a point several miles from the river. Only during recent weeks had their track

tunnels merged with the course of the Wood to become recognizable hoofprints in the shallower snow that overlay the
river ice. Their daily movements had then slowed even more
as they attained the place where walking became easier, and
they had dallied on the gravel bars and in the deeper snow
of the swampy interspaces, but always staying within a few
short steps of the Wood.

Then, in the rapidly approaching dusk, both animals had
bedded on an open bar, their backs to the wall of brush that
subtended it and more than a hundred yards apart. Earlier,
the cow had watched a wolverine as he worked his impatient way among the snow-buried deadfalls on the river's
opposite bank, but if the solitary animal scented her he gave
no sign of it and had soon disappeared from view.

Less than a mile separated the wolves from the calf and
cow, yet it was a distance too far for scent to travel on the
brittle, windless air. The pack continued to move downriver
and in loose formation, becoming invisible as the wolves
traversed the deep shadows beneath the river's cutbanks.
Then they emerged once more upon the open snow, slats of
soft moonlight rippling along their backs as they continued
to follow the snaking course of the frozen river.

A short time later, with the gray bitch leading, the wolves
entered a long loop in the stream's course, a place where it
doubled back upon itself. It was here that the old female
caught the scent of the calf, and as they gathered around
her the rest also learned of its nearness.

After touching noses with her big mate, the gray bitch
swung abruptly toward the narrow band of riverbar that
still separated her from the growing scent source. The rest
paused on the snow-covered ice before quickly following,
their tails erect and wagging excitedly.

The calf had heard the wolves even before he became
alert to the small snuffling sounds their noses made as they
appraised his scent where it layered outward under the cold

air. After staring in the direction of the unfamiliar sounds, he swung his head, looking toward the distant cow as if already sensing that she was too far from him in a potentially dangerous situation. Finally, flicking his oversize ears, he rose rump-first from the snow.

The young moose had already turned and taken several tentative steps in the direction of the cow when he saw the blurred shadow that was the black wolf. The big male had shouldered past his mate, and no waiting had accompanied his rush as weak moonlight showed him the calf's silhouette.

Striking heavily from the side and front, his jaws closed over the calf's muzzle, causing the moose to stagger sideways into the dense willows nearby, dragging his attacker with him. Then, though the big wolf's leap had been a successful one, he was raked by the tangled brush and felt his hold weaken and disappear as he rolled clumsily in the deep softness of the snow.

The panicked calf turned and lunged toward the open riverbar, still seeking the cow, and in doing so ran headlong into the rest of the pack.

This was unlike the nonviolent confrontation which the calf had experienced on that warm night during the autumn before. He was now blinded by the instinctive certainty that he was in grave danger. As he plunged wildly toward the distant cow, his nose was filled with the vaguely familiar scent of the intruders he knew so little about. So great was his fear that he felt only a staggering numbness as the wolves closed on his hindquarters before he slipped and fell heavily in the deep snow. As he struggled to rise he was unaware that the wolves no longer tore at his body, and as the cow towered over him a flooding weariness of shock made him abandon his attempt to regain his feet.

The long fast the wolves had endured made the exhaustion produced by their attack on the calf more difficult to dispel. Consequently, considerable time passed before they began slowly to move into the familiar half circle that, once formed, fenced the cow and calf against the wall of willow brush along the bar's rearmost edge.

Moisture from the heavy breathing of moose and wolves mingled with that which issued from the calf's open abdomen, and a thin layer of vapor gathered to hang oppressively in the brittle-cold air.

The calf died quietly after lying with its neck outstretched on the snow during the long hours that preceded the late dawn. Blood loss and shock had taken their toll while the cold sapped what strength remained after the brief but deadly struggle, but the cow continued to stand over her stricken calf until well after the light returned. Then she walked slowly along the willow fringe and crossed the frozen river, her retreat making the wolves rise to sitting positions, but they did not follow.

Though extremely hungry, and possibly because they were still recuperating from the heavy exertion that had been required to consummate the kill, the wolves fed slowly, with little of the usual minor bickering over choice spots on the carcass. As they consumed the still-warm meat, a solitary jay watched from a vantage point a few feet away. Finally, less than an hour after the feeding had begun, it ended as each wolf became gripped in an almost lethargic weariness and sought out a place in which to doze. The jay hopped boldly onto the carcass to pick at the solidifying tallow that overlay the calf's rump as the noon sun once more began to slip beneath the foglike layer of ice crystals that blanketed the desolate flats.

The cow had moved into a small clearing behind the belt of spruce that bordered the river's opposite bank. There, almost within hearing of the feeding pack, she stopped and began to browse among the frost-brittle shrubs that clustered above the surface of the deep snow. The memory of her calf was already fading, and as she moved slowly to find

more of the willow, she was vaguely aware of the dull,
cramping pains that filled her belly. To still them, she swung
her big head and nipped at her dark flanks. The cramps
were the only sign she would have as the calf in her uterus
aborted.

After staying within a quarter mile of the calf for nearly
five days, the St. George Creek pack left its remains to the
ravens. With the pack's departure, January became a reality.
Little daily change in the sustained cold continued to attend
the passing days, and the flats remained locked away beneath the snow, held there by temperatures that approached
sixty degrees below zero during the quiet nights. Though it
was an imperceptible process, with the passage of the solstice, the days were once more increasing in length, but the
addition of a few minutes to each twenty-four-hour period
provided no visible signal that winter was half over.

Through this monotony of cold the black led the seven
wolves almost to the place where the Wood joined the
broad, wind-scoured roughness of the Tanana River. Here
he once more swung toward the far-off mountains, and, following the obscure Tatlanika River, began yet another
seventy-mile traverse of the flats.

CHAPTER 19

The cable snares were invisible where they hung loop-like above the snow-covered track paths near the partially exposed remains of the Tatlanika River kill. They had been placed there by the old man with infinite care born of long experience, and they rested lightly over willow whips. The whips, in turn, rested in the forks made by lower branches of other bushes nearby. The hanging loops bridged most of the trails to the carcass at a height of about three feet. Crusted with rime frost, the seemingly innocuous steel loops had long ago assumed the identity of the willow thicket in which they waited.

Ten of the snares had been strategically placed by Tatum several weeks earlier, and all were well away from the remains of the kill and encircled it. Beneath them, and to the side of the trails over which the snares hung, lay the attached anchors, or drags, their hooklike steel grapples also dusted with frost and snow, making them invisible.

On the morning the old man had set the kill, he had once more debated the wisdom of using only the snares or supplementing them with two or three of the big number 114s. In practice, he considered mixing traps at a site such as that occupied by the remains of the bull a somewhat useless venture, one that sounded good when part of a trapping yarn, but which seldom produced results.

For the old man, the decision to set certain types of traps in specific places was an important one, for it related to the economics of wolf trapping. Once placed, each device represented a potential reward of several hundred dollars, the monetary worth of a prime pelt. The old man's needs throughout the year were simple, and could be filled by the revenue produced by the sale of even a half-dozen prime wolf skins. This fact and his lifelong fascination with the big predators were high on the list of reasons that Jake Tatum resided in the Tatlanika River country each winter and sought the wolves that shared it with him.

The tracks that he studied closely upon reaching the kill had told him with complete certainty that the pack boasted several young wolves. Because of this, and on impulse, he had decided to set some of the big spring traps along with the snares, and what was left of the short day slipped by unnoticed as the old man worked. Wearing the cotton gloves, he meticulously hung the snares, making each set only after a final study of the location it would occupy. Finally, his fingers numb where they had once been badly frostbitten, he moved to the protruding rib cage of the bull and dug three shallow holes near its mouth.

One of the bull's massive femur bones was frozen solidly into the hard-packed snow, and to this he secured the free ends of the heavy chains attached to the steel traps with heavy rust-coated wire. In shallow grooves he buried the chains and finally the set traps, but only after slipping a piece of crumpled wax paper under one jaw and over its mate on the opposite side of each trap. Last, he carefully sprinkled powder snow over the buried traps and chains, brushing the surface lightly with a small spruce branch. Stepping back a dozen yards, he surveyed his work, reset a nearby snare, and then walked across the river to the snowmobile. Sitting on the bare platform once occupied by the padded seat, he smoked before carefully snuffing the butt in his mittened hand and dropping it into his pocket. Then, in near darkness, he cranked life into the snowmobile, and started for the cabin.

In the days that followed, the old man observed the kill from a distance, usually from a vantage point along the side of the spruce-laced ridge that rose well away from the opposite riverbank. The trail he used was a looplike part of the main route of travel he had broken, and along this were set the rest of his traps. The trail covered more than twenty miles, and eventually returned to the cabin from upriver. He had used the venerable snowmobile to pack the deep snow, and almost two weeks had been required to finish the loop. Once made, however, packing caused the trail to harden, and each trip across it was easier than the last.

The main trail turned back in the direction of the cabin in the low hills to the southwest, and from this point assumed a different appearance than that of its first half. As the old man drove the snowmobile along the trail shortly after establishing it, he had left it at frequent intervals. These looping detours served a specific purpose.

Years of trapping had proved to Tatum that wolves liked to walk upon the trails he left, either out of curiosity or, more likely, because they made travel easier in the deep snow. Then through long observation, the old man had refined this knowledge. Trapwise wolves, he knew, often the bearers of less than the normal number of toes on their feet, and possessors of an uncanny knowledge where set traps were concerned, were also suspicious of such trails. These animals would, Tatum had observed, swing onto side trails rather than travel the main, more direct route.

By the end of January's first week, the old man had set most of the looping detour trails with what were called blind sets. These consisted of spring traps buried under the

trail's surface at random locations. The old man had cursed
colorfully as he gouged his knees while crawling over the
traps that rode on the sled behind him. From its rear, he
made the blind sets without standing on the ground, a
refinement that kept his own scent from betraying the traps'
locations.

Many trappers marked such sets with wisps of red survey
tape or yarn, but the old man disdained the method, preferring to rely upon his excellent memory when he checked the
trapline. The "blind" sets in the detour trails had been made
where they swung close to the main trail, often making a detour to check them unnecessary.

By mid-January, the old man was convinced that the valley of the Tatlanika was devoid of wolves. He had tarped off
the end of the cabin farthest from the stove, and in the cool
darkness beyond the canvas hung the fruits of his labors
thus far. A dozen fox pelts, one a silver male, added a musk
to the room and hung bundled flatly on a rusty nail which
protruded through the eyehole of each. Nearby, the plews of
eight lynx represented the best of the old man's catch from a
monetary point of view, though all but two were of average
size. A large wolverine pelt was still turned hair side in over
a smooth stretcher frame. It would hang this way for only a
few days, enough time for the air to partially dry the skin.
Then it would be turned hair side out and stored in the
coolness behind the tarp. Finally, almost two dozen marten
pelts added their mahogany richness to the catch.

The marten were considered by the old man to be almost
a diversion from the rigors of maintaining the long trail.
Most were taken within a mile of the cabin in the big spruce
which bordered the Tatlanika. The small tree-dwelling marten required little skill to catch, and with maturity reached a
length of about eighteen inches. Resembling their close
cousin the mink, they differed in that their pelts consisted of
finer, longer hair. Good marten pelts were almost black, and

most of the animals in Tatum's catch met this criteria. In addition, and regardless of predominant pelt color, each bore the peculiar throat and belly markings of rusty orange fur, which contrasted sharply with the rest of the pelt.

The old man often chuckled to himself over the fact that if curiosity killed the cat, it was even more deadly where the long-bodied marten were concerned. All that was required to bring one to the small traps he wired to the upper surfaces of deadfall poles and trees was a bit of Christmas tree tinsel, a feather, or a wisp of yarn, along with a small square of frozen moose hide. The added "bait" was simply hung beyond the exposed trap, and the marten, in his apparently unbridled curiosity, would literally crawl over the set to see the object that had captured his attention.

In the long darkness of the midwinter weeks, the Yukon stove ticked and squeaked as it gave up its heat to warm the cabin. The pungent scent of burning spruce splits and the pleasant yeastiness of others stacked along the wall near the stove permeated the cabin's interior and all that it held.

The husky preferred the crude plywood shelter the old man had erected along the cabin's rear outer wall. Heavy-furred and grown accustomed to the cold after many winters, she panted heavily on those few occasions that Tatum brought her inside for company. She used the shelter only when the air temperature plunged well below the zero mark, normally preferring to curl up, nose under tail, on the snow. An old dog, she nonetheless seemed to be comfortable, and in the evenings Tatum talked to her through the logs that made the cabin's rear wall. The sound of his voice was always rewarded by her thumping tail.

When the husky had been a pup, she had been part of a sled team the old man kept. That was before the advent of snowmobiles and in retrospect, still struck Tatum as a simpler method of transportation. All ten of the dogs that had comprised the team had thrived upon the dried, reeking chum salmon they ate year-round, and like thousands of others, came by the name "fish burners" honestly.

The husky's presence, rather than the dog herself, was company for the old man, despite the fact that the four fifty-pound bags of commercial dog meal had made a load that required an extra trip for the little airplane. Tatum hauled it each year because it was less bulky than the bales of fish.

The old man checked his main trapline each week. He had stayed in the cabin only during one five-day stretch when the red mercury in the thermometer outside slipped below its lowest mark of minus sixty degrees and rose only to minus thirty or forty during the short days. He had seen no wolf sign. Because of the age-induced necessity of traveling slowly, even on the snowmobile, a full day was required for each traverse of the line.

The trip started several hours before the late dawn and ended well after sunset. To keep warm in the bitter cold, Tatum wore a heavy down-insulated parka with a wolf-fur hood ruff. Down quilted leggings held up by brace suspenders completed his outerwear, and his feet stayed comfortable in knee-length moosehide mukluks. His moosehide boots were of the soft-soled Athabascan style, with beaver-fur trim around their tops. Clipped caribou hide made insoles which insulated their bottoms, and Tatum dreaded the day they would wear out, for they had been given to him by his wife. Gauntlet mittens hung by shoulder cords kept the old man's gnarled fingers reasonably warm between bouts with the balky snowmobile and the chore of resetting traps with only the protection of thin cotton gloves.

With the passage of time, and because there appeared to be no wolves using the river valley, the set near the kill assumed a low priority to the old man, and he did not check it during late January. Then warm air rode a rising wind, and a mantle of stringy clouds had shut out the sun. In the day's last light, Tatum had read an honest zero degrees on the thermometer, and later, sipping coffee, he decided to visit the kill the next day and pull the traps and snares.

CHAPTER 20

During the days in which she fed upon the carcass of the bull calf, the gray bitch had felt the first stirrings of unrest that signaled the approach of her breeding season. In response, she had initiated brief play periods with the black, and he had responded, though with less enthusiasm than hers. She dozed nearer to him than was her custom and, on occasion, rolled before him as he stood stiff-legged, his great dun-colored tail wagging slowly. It was a time of early courtship, yet it was doubtful that either wolf recognized it for what it was. Many weeks were yet to pass before the old female's vulva once more became swollen and the residual blood in her urine foretold her approaching readiness to breed.

The process of fasting began once more as the pack struck out to the south across the flats. As they traveled, a few rabbits were caught during each day but provided small nourishment. The renewed socialization and play that had occurred briefly while the wolves were well fed dwindled in the face of their recurring hunger.

The deep snow also took its toll, and the process of breaking trail became an exhausting chore, one which usually fell to the huge black and his one remaining adult son. As the pack reached the halfway point in its journey across the vast flats, the terrain opened and travel became somewhat easier. Even here, however, the common trail of the wolves often bore pink tinges from bleeding feet cut by razor-sharp ice along the ridged and wind-hardened surface of the upper Tatlanika River.

When the pack finally closed with the foothills of the Alaska Range, its members were once more gaunted, and traveled almost robotlike in single file and at a slow trot. Moose were scarce in this, the center, portion of the pack's range, though the wolves found several along the course of the lower Tatlanika River shortly after reaching it. The deep snow, a minor disadvantage to the huge browsers, slowed the pack, making it virtually impossible to press a successful attack. On two occasions the wolves had been offered the sought-after opportunity to close with moose from the rear, and each time had been simply outrun by their quarry.

As the pack moved higher along the course of the Tatlanika, the country opened even more. The silent river channels were many and separated by narrow willow-choked islands, each encased by stark hoarfrost. Beneath their white crowns, the scrubby plants were girdled where snowshoe hares had eaten the bark and exposed the yellow-white underwood. Their tracks were networked along the margin of each willow clump and crosscrossed the open river channels between adjacent islands.

Still following the river and as they approached the lower tip of such islands, the pack fanned out in line-abreast formation. Then without stopping, they broke into a ground-eating run which quickly carried them through the narrow stands of dense willow. Many of the white hares learned of the pack's coming too late. After several panicked leaps ahead of the nearest wolf, they instinctively dodged either right or left, a course which often took them directly into the path of the next wolf.

During the several days the pack spent climbing the last

gradient leading to the mouth of the Tatlanika Valley where the river emerged from the mountains, a number of rabbits were taken. One of the male pups was successful on several occasions, but each time surrendered his kill to the buff-colored wolf.

All three of the old female's pups were in critical need of food. The odd mouthful of rabbit they had managed to bolt had added nothing to their weight. They were proportionately thinner than the rest of the pack members because in addition to maintaining themselves during the deep cold they were still growing. Each showed well-defined rib outlines beneath the skin and hair that covered their chests and sides. They were, in fact, suffering early stages of true starvation.

Adding to the effects of an almost total lack of nourishment was the accompanying exhaustion. Each day the pups tired faster than they had during the day preceding and they began to lag behind the moving pack. Rest periods for the adults became more frequent but did the pups little good, for more often than not, they caught up just as the leader struck out once more for the towering mountains ahead.

As always, there was the deep, bone-numbing cold. Where once comfort could be found by simply curling up on the snow with noses tucked under their tails, the pups now rested little. Rising often to turn before curling up once more, they shivered violently in half-sleep, and because they too suffered from the lack of food, the adults rested little during their frequent nap periods and rest stops, which became even shorter as the days passed.

The St. George Creek pack entered the mouth of the Tatlanika Valley under a high overcast sky and during mid-afternoon on a day when the air temperature had risen dramatically. Perhaps because of the warmth he felt in the gusting wind that ruffled his shoulder roach, the big wolf increased his pace, and as full darkness descended over the frozen river the pack reached a point less than a mile below the remnants of the Tatlanika kill. It was here that the black's nose caught the faint pungency of wood smoke, which rode the air currents that flowed from the upper valley, and as he stopped to sample the wind with his nose, the rest of the pack bunched around him to seek the source of the scent that all but the three young pups had experienced many times before.

Though the black wolf and his gray mate were incapable of drawing a conscious comparison, there was a familiar sameness to the smoke scent, like that which they experienced when the forests burned during the warm part of each year, but less musty and rank.

The wind-winnowed scent pockets bore a cleaner smell, possibly hinting at a dry warmness that the black somehow sensed more strongly than did the others. Perhaps because of this, the smell held an attraction for him which stimulated a desire to move closer to its as yet unidentified source. He nuzzled his mate's shoulder as she moved past him to trot tentatively ahead, holding her head high as she tested the constancy of the scent. She too felt the attraction that the smoke held, and it is possible that it caused her to raise her muzzle and howl, the long, quavering note muffled among the snow-burdened spruces.

The bitch howled once more, this time joined by her female pup, and followed closely by the black and the others. A quarter-moon washed the dark slopes that defined the valley, making vague silhouettes of the ridges before once more slipping behind the low clouds. As the pack moved slowly up the frozen river, a faint nervousness replaced the vague familiarity instilled by the smoke scent, which grew stronger as the pack ascended the drainage. The black sensed this too, and his movements became more erratic and hesitant as he followed the river course. The snow cover here was shallow, and he moved steadily, often dropping back to the rear to pause and watch the pack's back trail. At such times, the night noises occasionally caused him to flinch and sidestep before moving on.

Even had the river not moved toward it, the wolves would have followed the smoke scent to its source. That the wind which carried it moved from an upstream direction was merely a coincidental convenience, and faint cream-colored light stained the eastern horizon as the black stopped once more near a jumble of rock and bleached spruce snags that had built in the riverbed during the spring before. Licking snow, he flopped down in the lee of the brush jam to lick the most recent of the cuts on his massive paws. The rest of the pack followed his lead, their shallow panting clicking softly in their throats.

Six ravens had fed upon the remnants of the Tatlanika kill when they were still fresh. With abandonment by the pack, they had enjoyed relatively free access to what little the wolves had left. Only a goshawk vied with them for small scraps that were carried into the trees by the ravens, but the otherwise fierce bird of prey was driven off amid numerous nonviolent confrontations and much ruffling of neck feathers. Even their broad and powerful black beaks, however, had been incapable of penetrating the half-inch thick skin that still covered the space between the bull's small antlers, but the moose's eyes and the soft parts of his lips had been another matter, and the black scavengers had made quick work of both. Then with the coming of the deep cold the ravens had gone elsewhere to skillfully seek food for their own survival.

Now, the same warming that attended the pack's return to the Tatlanika caused the ravens' most recent stopover at the old kill during the first weak light of morning. The birds had also followed the river's course from its beginnings at the cleft in the foothills where it exited the range, and the flock's passage overhead had been marked only by the luffing of wings on the gusting wind. Reaching the kill, they had circled it before perching among the spruce tops above it, clucking and piping resonantly among themselves.

At first they were content to enjoy the feeble warmth of the rising sun that tipped the high spruces. Then one of the flock, a young bird, launched herself and spiraled lazily downward to alight on one of the smallish antler palms where it protruded through the snow.

Cocking her bristled head and flaring her ebony wings for balance, she uttered a guttural croak before sidestepping along the slippery edge of the antler and finally hopping down onto the dusting of snow that covered the skull itself. Several more ungainly hopping steps took her into the shadow of the rib cage, and as she reached it a second bird dropped from its perch in the spruces to join her. It was still seeking a place to alight when the first bird stepped onto the concealed pan of one of the big traps beneath the snow.

Because of the bird's light weight, the jaws missed its body while closing upon and effortlessly shattering the hollow leg bones. It flopped awkwardly, unable to move the heavy Newhouse trap, while its high-pitched distress calls were answered by the others in the spruces above.

A quarter mile downriver, the wolves heard the raucous chorus, and something in its tenor made the pack stop and listen attentively. The calling of ravens often meant that they had discovered a band of caribou or a moose bedded in the sun along an open hillside, an event which usually provided a diversion for the birds in the form of an opportunity to harass the hapless victim.

In full light now, the big pack leader rose and shook himself. Still listening to the clamoring ravens, he stretched and lapped idly at the granular snow before moving slowly off in an upstream direction, followed by the rest of the pack.

The wolves would have found the trap-caught bird even

had it not flapped its wings in a last exhausted effort to free itself from the trap. Musky feather scent and the fainter richness of fresh blood ran in a shallow layer onto the river-bed and was carried easily by the wind to the approaching wolves. It is doubtful that, when she spotted the pinioned carrion eater, the gray bitch recognized the place for what it was, or interpreted the strange actions of the bird.

Stopping short while still fifty yards from the raven, she sat down on the snow to watch. There was an unnatural quality in the scene before her, and it confused her. Her pups had already initiated a stalk upon the weakly flopping bird, satisfaction of their curiosity and hunger being quick goals that stifled caution. They were followed closely by the buff male and one of the white bitches. The black wolf had circled the kill, and holding his head high, stood watching from the open riverbar above it.

The big male pup launched his clumsy attack from a distance of ten yards, an attack that ended abruptly in a scream of surprised pain as his right front paw triggered the second of the three Newhouse traps. The raven forgotten, he leaped high in the air and then lunged forward, where he was tumbled by the trap's drag chain.

The second male pup, the small gray female, and the buff wolf were close behind when the trap closed. In the moments that followed, the second male pup and the buff wolf veered to the left and plunged into the willows behind the kill, where both animals ran headlong into separate snares. The small female stopped dead in her tracks while still a half-dozen feet from her stricken brother, and it was this that probably saved her life.

The resident female narrowly missed yet another snare as she plunged through the willow thicket to the steep hillside behind the bar. Continuing up the slope, she did not hesitate to look back as she topped the ridge and disappeared from sight.

With the pup's first cry, the black and his mate were running flat-out and downriver, followed closely by the second resident female. The big leader and the gray bitch veered into the spruces and slowed only after a quarter of a mile separated them from the kill. The second resident bitch continued downriver before she too dodged into the willows on the far side of the river.

Both the buff male and the gray bitch's pup died shortly after they encountered the snares. They were held securely around the neck and fought the choking cable, which, once tightened, retained its lethal grip. Suffocation followed soon after the drags caught solidly in the tangled willows. They died soundlessly.

The first pup was not so fortunate. Numbness quickly replaced the momentary agony produced by the closing trap jaws, and the young wolf found himself secured to the frozen carcass of the kill at which he had once fed. He quickly found that he could exert pressure on the shock-deadened foot held in the trap, and he lunged heavily in a futile effort to escape. Two of the ravens returned to watch cautiously from a perch in the top of a dead spruce snag across the river as he began to chew on the heavy trap, the sounds of his teeth scraping metallically in the quiet produced by the dying wind gusts.

CHAPTER 21

The old man had seen hundreds of wolves during the long years and the tracks of perhaps a thousand more. Squatting now, he slipped the mitten from his right hand and spanned one of the big prints for size. His whispered proclamation attested to the track's width as his eyes followed the line of prints to the point at which they disappeared over a low cutbank that was topped by small spruce and willow, and into the blue shadows beyond.

The black wolf had been followed closely by his smaller mate as he fled the pandemonium at the old kill. His flight had taken him upriver along the ridge crest which paralleled the Tatlanika, where panic had slowly given way to nervous apprehension and finally to the intense curiosity which had caused both wolves to hesitantly descend once more to the river and cross it less than a quarter of a mile below the cabin.

Though he had seen traps in the past, and had quickly learned to find by their appearance and scent those that were poorly set, the big wolf was not capable of defining the sudden loss and absence of his buff son and the two young pups. Their disappearance created a frustrating nervousness coupled with a fear of the place where he had last seen them.

The gray bitch limped as she followed the big wolf, the pain in her hind leg and hip possibly stemming from the same nervous association with the stark suddenness and unnatural quality she sensed in the chaos that had erupted at the kill or, more probably, from the exertion she had expended during the lunging escape.

Her own track line paralleled that of the black, but the old man scarcely glanced at it as he continued downriver toward the old kill. Then, as he turned the last bend above it, he spotted the dun pup sitting upright against the bull's rib cage, and he momentarily forgot the big tracks he had seen.

The pup had heard the approaching snowmobile. It was a sound he had never heard before, and as it grew, it had caused him to lunge once more to the end of the trap's drag chain, where, as countless times before, he had been rudely somersaulted onto the well-packed snow. Finally, as he watched the old man dismount on the openness of the riverbed, his broken teeth chattered softly and he trembled violently.

Shutting the machine off and with rifle in hand, the old man approached the wolf slowly. The pup faced his adversary, and as the distance between the two shortened, the pup rose and took a step forward while slowly wagging his tail as if in greeting. The old man had seen this strange ritual on many other occasions, yet had never ceased to wonder why a trapped wolf often seemed almost eager to meet the only creature he truly feared. The ritual's repetition had put the lie to the old wives' tale which depicted snarling wolves at bay.

The small-caliber bullet ended the dun pup's life even before the muffled pop of the gun reached his upturned ears, and only then did the old man begin studying the track sign around the kill. He quickly found the already stiffening carcasses of the buff wolf and the other blue-gray pup where they lay partly covered with powder snow among the willows. Tatum dragged the three wolves to the snowmobile before returning to the kill to more leisurely examine the profusion of tracks that laced the willows and open snow around it.

Working back onto the open riverbed, the old man accurately counted the pack's number, and by deduction, its survivors. Once more, he marveled at the size of the big track set that reversed itself on the open snow long before reaching the place where his traps had been concealed, then led back upon itself in fifteen-foot bounds toward the opposite bank of the Tatlanika.

The old man knew that with their discovery, the traps near the remains of the moose had been rendered useless, and that the wolves would not return. So he set to work collecting his snares, and as he dug up the steel traps, the last of which had been sprung by the pup's efforts to escape, he read the story told by the dead raven.

A short time later, with the bodies of the three wolves loaded in the small collapsible sled he pulled behind the snowmobile, Tatum headed back upriver toward the cabin. Along the way, he stopped only once to make a three-trap blind set in the machine's corrugated back trail. His mind, however, was on other things, namely the wolf that had made the big tracks, an animal that was obviously a prominent member of the pack he was yet to see.

As he completed the set, the old man watched the first snowflakes begin to fall. They were not unexpected, for the cloud cover and the warmed air temperatures that accompanied it had been sure signs. Later, as he reached the cabin, the spruce across the river were already blurred behind a heavy curtain of falling flakes, and as he skinned the wolves, yellow lantern light spilled through the small window to offer the only spot of brightness in a world once more gone dark and silent.

❧ CHAPTER 22

The black wolf thrust his muscular body forward as he broke trail in the deep snow that mantled the slope a mile behind the cabin, the long guard hairs on his back matted with moisture where the newly falling flakes melted. The gray bitch followed in his tunnel-like path, her panting interspersed with an almost inaudible whining, the result of the cramping pain in her gimped leg.

The pair had traveled a broad circle, the farthest edge of which had cut the Tatlanika well above the site of the old kill. The absence of the rest of the pack had deepened the nervous loneliness which gripped both wolves, though only five hours had passed since the trap had closed on the dun pup's foreleg. Their movements were merely random wanderings controlled only by an unrecognizable reluctance to stray too far from the last place at which the pack had been together.

The gray bitch's small female pup had recovered her senses even as the first shrill scream of her trapped brother died in her ears. Then she had whirled and plunged blindly into the willows nearby, a course which followed the same path taken by the buff male only moments before. As she leaped clear of him where he struggled in the choking noose, she narrowly missed being caught by a second snare nearby. Then, clear of the kill, she overtook the white resident bitch as the latter slowed among the shadows beneath the dark spruces that bordered the river.

After separating from the black and his mate, the second white wolf had plunged farther downriver. Beyond the brush of the riverbank, she entered a tiny, deep-cut gully made by a feeder stream which fed into the Tatlanika. Climbing until exhaustion made her stop among the root snags and boulders which choked its upper limits, she finally rested, panting heavily in the gloom which preceded the new snow that had already begun to fall. Then she had continued up the steep grade of the stream, following its convolutions until they merged with the open ridge far above the river.

The St. George Creek pack now consisted of five scattered members. Its ranks had been further depleted not only in number, however, but in over-all strength, for with the loss of the second buff male, the black would be critically hampered in his ability to hunt moose during that time of the year when the strength of numbers among wolves is most vital.

During the night that followed the incidents at the kill, the falling snow thickened in the velvet darkness. The black wolf felt its cold wetness along his broad muzzle as he stopped on the barren, windless ridgetop that he and his mate had followed since they had fled the river. It was here, just above the stunted spruce thickets that marked the lower edges of the open slopes above, that he howled.

The deep resonance of the big wolf's call, muffled in the silent grayness of falling snow, was repeated several times before the gray bitch joined in with her shorter, higher-pitched notes. Then, as the black swiveled his ears forward to listen, he heard the almost inaudible answering howl that floated from among the blanket of trees far behind and below him. He recognized the gray female pup in the faint sound.

An hour later, the black and his mate shared a happy reunion with their last surviving pup as they met along the spine of the ridge's lower reaches. The white resident female did not share in the muzzle grasping and rolling, but stood aside, her only indication of happiness evidenced by the slow wagging of her tail.

The second white resident did not hear the calling of the others. After her escape from the river she had topped the series of ridges to the west of the valley, then continued to drop lower among the foothills beyond. Traveling alone, she had kept to the brushy gullies that veined the land and, perhaps because of this, the distant voices of the others went undetected. With the coming of dawn, she was five miles from the rest of the pack.

As the month of February reached its final weeks, periodic but short moderations in the weather occurred, and during the final week a thaw caused the winter's accumulation of snow on the limbs of the spruces to fatten with melting water. The added weight and its concentration caused the needle-dense branches to bend, and finally release their burden before snapping upright once more. Canada jays reappeared as if by magic to glide among the openings, their calls merging with the belling rasps of congregating ravens. The warmth in the still air was, however, a false promise and did little more than mark the final constriction of winter's grasp upon the land. As a result, and with the arrival of March, the bitter cold returned as if to prove that the sixty days to come would once more represent that time of the year when survival would be dependent not only upon skill but simple good fortune.

Separated from the others, the white bitch owed her life to the periods of midwinter warmth that February had produced, along with the rabbits she was fortunate to catch.

Simple coincidence, which followed on the heels of the panicked escape from the traps at the Tatlanika kill, had caused the main pack and the white bitch to take opposing courses of travel, and the distance that finally separated them exceeded fifteen miles.

After the reunion on the ridge, the black had picked a route which swung abruptly to the east and away from the Tatlanika Valley. Like the single white resident, the big leader and the three wolves that followed him became dependent once more upon the long-legged rabbits that ghosted among the spruce draws, and their survival was also enhanced by the warmer days that had thawed the snow among the foothills during February's final weeks.

With the loss of the buff male and the two inexperienced pups, the strength in numbers that defined the pack's ability to kill its prey had decreased dangerously. This fact, added to the wolves' generally poor physical condition, made the hunting of moose a frustrating and wholly unsuccessful venture. And far from the least of the handicaps that now plagued the pack was the persistent lameness that caused the old gray bitch to limp badly as she brought up the rear of the moving group.

Though still a unit of four, and to the eyes of a casual observer healthy, the St. George Creek pack was literally fighting for its life. Eash passing day and the travel required to take whatever advantage might come during the exploration of new hunting territory further eroded the reserves of energy each wolf possessed, reserves which withered steadily, even while fed by the pale and stringy flesh of many rabbits.

On several occasions the big black had found moose, the most recent having been a pair of mature cows that were wintering in an obscure creek drainage several miles to the west of the Tatlanika. The charge, which had been immediate, failed miserably as the moose stood their ground in the deep snow and alder tangles. Alone in the effort, exhausted, and as if sensing the futility of the venture, the black had quit after his second rush. The pack stayed in the vicinity of the cows for several days, during which they watched both animals from a distance. Finally the black moved on, the others strung out along the trail he broke in the crusted snow of the wind-scoured drainage.

Then, during a windy night, the single resident bitch cut the two-day-old trail left by the main pack. Though there was little of their scent remaining in the drifted track tunnel, she swung into the pack's trail. By evening of the following day, she had caught up, and after a few brief minutes of circling by the big leader and his mate, during which the white female rolled onto her side in the snow, she was accepted back.

The five wolves spent the early weeks of March among the low slopes of the range well to the west of the place where the Tatlanika River exited the mountains' foothills. Following ridgetops and scree slopes, the black found nothing to eat and eventually climbed higher above the spruce-studded valleys that bordered the desolate flats. It was this leg of the pack's journey that led to a bit of luck that provided its salvation.

The band of Dall sheep was a small one and was composed of less than a dozen ewes, two half-curl rams, and a pair of knob-kneed lambs that the group had brought with it from the high slopes above the place called Buzzard Creek.

During the autumn past, the flock had grazed upon the mosses, lichens, and red ground willow that carpeted the meadows in the higher elevations, but with the coming of the snows they had been pushed inexorably downward in search of nourishment. The deepening of the snow over the preferred alpine meadows had quickly made digging for food an impractical venture and, finally, by late February the sheep had taken up residence among the desolate willow draws of Buzzard Creek. It was here that the wolves found them.

Having topped a barren ridge, and feeling the wind push against him, winnowing the long blue-black mane hairs along his powerful back and neck, the black paused to survey the valley below. The weather had once more warmed, and the rise in the air's temperature was accompanied by an increase in its ability to hold and carry scent. It was, however, the big wolf's eyes that told him of the sheeps' location first as he studied the rutted network of deep trails the band had left in the cleftlike valley below.

The sheep were bedded among the willows, and thus invisible to the wolves even from their vantage point on the ridgetop. After descending a short distance, the pack milled around the black, wagging their tails excitedly as the first wash of scent built and then declined under the influence of the gusting wind that ran upslope toward them.

Well below the crest, the black broke a zigzag trail as he descended the slope, scattering a small avalanche of snow which tumbled ahead of him, and the pack had halved the distance separating sheep and wolves before an old ewe saw them. Having paused briefly, the black saw the movement as the band stood as one to watch the approaching pack.

The kill that followed was an easy one. The sheep, though in good health, were at a terrible disadvantage in the deep snow of the narrow gully. Denied the natural safety they would have sought by climbing swiftly among the rocks and debris of the slope above them, their only avenue of escape lay in the gully itself, and the soughing wind carried their bleats and grunts as the pack closed quickly.

The black required only a few seconds following the start of his attack to drag one of the sickle-horned ewes down, and even as he did so, the gray bitch cut short the escape of another as the sheep lunged desperately into the deep snow of the slope.

The pack could easily have followed the survivors and decimated the band's numbers even further, but it did not. Perhaps the sudden presence of fresh meat stunted the desire to kill or, more likely, the expenditure of precious remaining energy had depleted the small reserves left to the wolves to the point where they could do no more. Whatever the reason, the pack was already feeding as the surviving sheep finally, free of deep snow, made good their laborious escape across the shale ridge that overlooked Buzzard Creek.

Two hundred pounds of deep-red meat, bluish sinew, pale-pink bone, and yellow-white hair were consumed by the pack in less than two days, and the scarlet stains that marked the place where the kill had been made darkened as they absorbed the light of the sun and, by heat absorption, melted the granular snow.

In actuality, the gray female's current heat period had begun more than a month before the pack's arrival at Buzzard Creek. Her urine had, even then, occasionally been flecked with the bright blood that was a harbinger of the time when she would be ready to breed with the black. Strangely, its presence had not changed or noticeably heightened the big wolf's interest in his mate during those early weeks. Then, under the strong influence of the necessary estrogenic hormones, her uterus once more prepared itself for ovulation, and the scent of her urine changed. This occurred during the week prior to the pack's success at Buzzard Creek, and it had been during that period that the black wolf's ardor had once more become a tangible entity. Finally, during the well-fed days at the sheep kill, he mounted her several times, and during the final copulation his still-virile sperm found several of the minute ova her heat had made available. As a result, when the pack swung upslope along the creek gully abandoning the scant remains

of its most recent success, the gray bitch was pregnant once
more.

During the first day after it had departed the austere
bleakness of Buzzard Creek, the pack's droppings were well
laced with white hair that had been consumed with other
less edible portions of the kill. The black continued to climb
the ridges that formed the drainage of the creek until, at an
elevation of more than 2,600 feet, he reached the place
where it ceased to exist. Swinging to the east, and trotting
tail-down in a horizontal layer of blowing snow, he led the
pack as it traversed a series of lesser ridges that spanned the
ten-mile distance to the extreme upper head of the Tatlanika River.

The pelts of the buff wolf and dun pups hung on stretcher
boards hair side out in the darkness at the rear of Jake Tatum's cabin. After collecting them from his traps, the old
man had not been surprised by the complete absence of
wolves from the valley, for it was expected. He had continued to work the trapline during the last days of February
and early March, adding regularly to the pile of nude
carcasses that were stacked in the snow near the cabin.
Then, on a warm day in mid-March, he once more cut the
trail of the big wolf that had been wise enough to stay clear
of the traps at the Tatlanika kill. With the discovery, he had
once more marveled at the size of the black's prints.

After crossing the final ridge, the big wolf had led the
pack down the steep, windswept tilt of Boulder Creek's
snow-encased bed to its junction with Roosevelt and Hearst
creeks, all obscure sources which combined to form the beginnings of the Tatlanika. Here the corniced snow which
hung from rock ledges and the blinding whiteness were devoid of life, even ravens, and the pack did not pause in its
passage. The return of the wolves at nightfall to the spruce

thickets several miles above the cabin was witnessed only by a large horned owl as the bird swiveled its tufted head downward to watch the wolves pass beneath its roosting tree along the river.

The white rabbits that had sustained the wolves by providing them with a scanty though fairly dependable source of food had represented a bounty for the owl. As the bird, a female, shifted along the polished limb upon which she roosted, the pale moon made momentary pinpoints of light in her large, unblinking eyes and grayed her back feathers while illuminating the scattered, cocoonlike pellets her digestive system had expelled on the snow beneath the big spruce. Consisting of hair and small bones, they were the result of her highly selective digestive process and the scant remnants of her feeding were especially plentiful beneath her favored roosts.

With the silent passage of the St. George Creek pack, the big bird had straightened on her perch, swiveled her head one last time, then stooped and glided without sound into the deep shadows that led to her large, stick-thatched nest. Alighting softly on its lip, she fluffed her soft feathers and resumed her vigil. Later she would leave once more to move among the spruce groves, where, from other temporary stopping places, she would watch for hares. Before dawn at least one would be crushed in her huge taloned claws, its wailing scream signaling her success. Then, her hunger sated, she would return to the nest that would hold two large off-white eggs before the snow thawed.

CHAPTER 23

Bright midmorning sunshine flooded the steep hillside in the spruce where the pack lay scattered among a jungle of deadfall timber and upturned root snags. The two white bitches were absent, and the black raised his head slowly to test the almost nonexistent breeze that washed the place. Only the faintest odors of spruce pitch and bark along with the slatelike scent of old snow were evident, and after several long minutes the big wolf tucked his long muzzle beneath his tail once more and closed his eyes.

The wolves had returned often to the tiny clearing since their last arrival in the valley of the Tatlanika. Well away from the river and almost four miles from the cabin of Jake Tatum, it was a place of natural concealment. The old man's travels took him well away from the pack's loafing place rather than nearer to it, and, as a result, his trails were concentrated on the valley floor to the west of the cabin.

With the slow passage of March and its final surrender to early April, the first real promises of warm weather became more frequent and genuine. The warming air produced white hoarfrost on the still-frozen and snow-free earth beneath undercut banks.

Close by the three sleeping wolves, translucent curls of bark were bright highlights along the trunks of birch as they picked up the sun glare behind them, and the spruces and dense alder thickets were alive with small birds, most of them winter residents. Chickadees, with their jaunty, jet-black caps, buzzed while nervously exchanging places on needle-dense limbs while slate-colored juncos flashed their stark-white tail feathers in swooping flight. Canada jays added their solemn calls as, in pairs, they too investigated the secret shadows beneath the brooding trees. Flights of Bohemian waxwings paused among the tops of leafless aspens and, higher along the crests of the sunlit hills, groups of the ever-present ravens tumbled and swooped, at play in the warming air.

The wolves had, in an almost unnoticeable manner, also changed their daily habit patterns. The tight-knit closeness that marked the interminable winter months had given way to more casual movements, as witnessed by the early departure of the resident bitches earlier that morning.

The old bitch had watched them take their leave from her resting place in a sun patch along the rotting spruce trunk where she lay even before the sun had truly begun to warm. They had stood, shaken the snow from their coats, urinated in turn, and then glided slowly downslope to disappear into the cobalt shadows at the clearing's lower edge.

The pack's renewed desire to sleep away the daylight hours was, in all probability, triggered by the returning sunlight. Diurnal periods were now more than twelve hours long, and with their rapidly burgeoning duration, the land's exposure to the higher sun brought a more permanent warmth that made long periods of idle dozing not only an enjoyable but profitable venture. Such idleness during the warm hours propagated conservation of the meager energy stores of winter.

To all outward appearances, survival for the black wolf and his followers seemed guaranteed now, but their still-cramped guts caused the dozing wolves to whimper and intermittently stretch their forelegs before once more slipping into an almost lethargic half-sleep. It was this forced wakefulness that had caused the two white females to leave the clearing that day, and this was the factor which brought them ultimately to the bank of the Tatlanika where they sat on the brilliance of open snow to watch the silent cabin of Jake Tatum.

Both wolves had gone there by choice rather than mere chance. While still a mile upriver, they had scented the thin haze of spruce smoke that scurled among the trees and washed the open snow of the river. At first the scent had been almost nonexistent, yet enough of it had been present to cause the pair to swing downriver toward its source. Then, as it strengthened, it built the strange warmth of attraction, and casual interest gave way to open curiosity.

The white wolves had closed to a point less than three hundred yards from the cabin, which was now clearly visible from their vantage point on the open snow of the river's opposite bank. As they watched, only the thin wisps of white smoke that issued from the rusted tin pipe chimney gave movement to the place, yet it was enough to hold their attention closely.

The distant belling of a raven intruded upon the silence and caused both wolves to pitch their ears forward while they continued to watch the smoke, which thinned visibly as the minutes passed. With the sun strengthening, several gray jays began to make patient sorties to the pile of frozen carcasses, flickering across a patchwork of sunny places on unmoving wings.

The minutes continued to slip away, and after retreating a short distance along their back trail, both wolves made a brief excursion onto the open ice of the river before once more returning to their watching place. Their initial apprehension slowly gave way to familiarity, and the pair finally crossed the open river to slip into the dense fringe of willow brush on the other side. It was here that they inadvertently discovered the airplane.

Approaching cautiously, they quietly sniffed the base of the drum that anchored one of the craft's wings, then shied away from some insignificant sound before slipping into the willows once more. The faint scents of engine oil and high-octane gasoline that had been brought to life in the warming air tingled in the noses of both wolves as they returned hesitantly to sample more of the scent.

Another half hour passed during which the white wolves lingered in and behind the security of the dense willow. Finally they began a cautious approach toward the cabin itself, but not before circling to its downwind side. As they slowly negotiated the clearing's edge, they encountered the abrupt curtain of heavy feral scent that drifted from the carcass pile, and they paused to fill their noses with the vaguely familiar but unidentifiable mix. Moving once more, and just beyond the snow-covered heap of the slowly decaying remains of the old man's efforts, they encountered the warmer scent of the old husky dog as she lay curled in late sleep in the shelter box.

Examining the new scent, both of the wolves, with slowly wagging tails, sat upright on the snow and faced the direction from which it came. Its density and warmth told them that its maker was nearby, and as if to offer proof, the dog shook herself, the chain which held her in the old man's absence tunking hollowly on the boards.

With the unexpected sound, both wolves stood and advanced slowly, their earlier caution diluted now by the increased scent and the sounds which accompanied it. Ten feet from the entrance to the husky's makeshift bed, they stopped and once more sat on the packed snow, their tails still wagging and their lolling tongues hidden behind the vapor plumes their breathing made.

Tatum's husky was an old dog, her pale blue eyes already

clouding with the milky blindness of senility. As she rose to stretch and shake, there was nothing to warn her of needed caution, and after yawning deeply, she stepped out into the bright sun, which momentarily blinded her.

The dog's appearance merely hastened the inevitable, and her failing eyes caught only blurred movement before she was knocked from her feet and quickly pinned by her throat on the snow. She died without sound beneath the weight of the white wolves, each of which outstripped her by more than thirty pounds. Then, as they attempted to drag her carcass away from the cabin, the chain which tethered it came tight, and the wolves fed on the spot. By midafternoon only the husky's head and half of its attached spinal column remained, made macabre by the still-attached collar and chain.

Long shadows lanced across the river snow as the late afternoon sun dropped lower behind the dense spruce near the cabin, and the air cooled quickly. After dozing several hundred yards away, both wolves stood and stretched their legs before returning to sniff the dog's pathetic remains. Then, turning, they walked slowly toward the river.

The old man had worried about the husky when he set the double-springed number-three traps near the base of the carcass pile. A wolverine had visited the place on several occasions while he was away, however, and at the time this seemed to justify a decision to set them. The traps had then lain beneath the building snow, and after several weeks the old man had forgotten them.

One of the white wolves paused to urinate as she passed the carcass pile, after which she swung toward it. As she reached for the intoxicating scent with her nose, the small trap closed upon her right forepaw. She made no outcry, but leaped straight into the air to be jerked rudely back to earth by the drag chain, which was firmly frozen where it was attached to the rock-hard trunk of a long-buried carcass.

The trap that imprisoned the white bitch was not a large one. It gripped less firmly than a bigger trap, and produced less of the numbing shock upon closure. Thus, with the passage of only a few minutes, excruciating pain quickly coursed upward into the white wolf's leg, making her whine and pant deeply. Each small movement she made against the hold and pull of the trap caused a cramping agony, which soon spread into her chest and forequarters. Instead of causing her to increase her efforts to break free, the pain rather than the mere mechanical holding strength of the trap caused her to crouch protectively over her crushed paw. She continued to whine raggedly as her sister watched from the deepening shadows.

Darkness was almost complete when the distant, popping drone of Tatum's snowmobile drifted into the trapped wolf's consciousness, and she paused in the licking of her forefoot to listen. Minutes later she sat upright to watch the approach of the machine's headlight as, seemingly disembodied, it cut a jerking, erratic path through the darkness.

The old man swung the machine across the riverbed, and as he topped the gentle slope on the cabin side of the river, the snowmobile's brilliant light caught the red glow of the white bitch's eyes.

Stopping, and with the machine at idle, Tatum slipped the heavy mitten from his right hand and reached slowly for the rifle that rode in a crude scabbard beneath his leg. Momentarily confused by the wolf's reluctance to flee, he remembered the traps moments before the rifle's pop extinguished the glowing eyes in the snow beyond. After dragging the body of the white bitch to the area of hard-packed snow near the entrance to the cabin, the old man lit a lantern and quickly built a fire in the Yukon stove. As his eyes became accustomed to the light, he cursed a small leak

in the roof that had, during the day, created a small stalag-
mite of clear ice on the table's worn oilcloth surface. Later,
perhaps tomorrow, he would scrape the thawing snow from
the roof and somehow repair it.

Sipping the scalding coffee and listening to the mind-
warming sounds made by the crackling spruce pitch in the
stove, he reflected upon his unexpected good fortune that
the white wolf had ventured so close to the cabin. Hunger
had obviously been the reason, and the carcass heap seemed
a reasonable goal for such needs. As the first warmth of the
stove pushed the wall of cold air ahead of it, the old man
spoke to the husky, and the unnatural quiet that followed
intruded slowly upon his wandering thoughts.

In the hissing pressure lantern's sterile light, the grim and
pathetic remains of the dog seemed to leap upward from the
snow at the old man's feet. He cursed bitterly before turning
back to the cabin. As he passed the stiffening carcass of the
white wolf, its well-distended belly seemed to mock the
hunger that brought it here, and seemed repulsive.

Despite his exhaustion, the old man sat in the circle of
lantern light long after the strips of moose he had hastily
thawed and fried had been eaten. The meat had tasted flat,
as did the whiskey he drank from the bottle before him, and
as he sat, the trapping of wolves took on a new aspect, one
of revenge. A plan drifted into the old man's numbed mind,
a plan which focused upon the red airplane that stood encased in the snow outside.

❧CHAPTER 24

Jake Tatum's life-style had irreversibly shaped his attitude about dogs and other property. During the long weeks that followed, what others would have been quick to label the outright and inexcusable murder of his husky dog merely rankled in the old man's thinking.

An incorrigible pragmatist, as were most others of his era, he had valued the almost neutral companionship the dog provided rather than the more sentimental attachment felt by those he disdained as city-bred pet lovers. Even so, there was a small degree of the latter, but the old man recognized its origin and repressed it in his thinking. As a pup, the dog had been a favorite of his wife.

Perhaps ironically, his long association with the animal that had caused the dog's death neutralized all but the nagging belief that he had simply been robbed. The killing had taken place well within the perimeter of that small part of the Tatlanika Valley that he had long ago pre-empted as his own, and like the destruction of the seat on the snowmobile, it insulted him deeply. In the end, he experienced the same hatred he felt toward men who vandalized and pilfered cabins such as his own, for they galled the old man's sense of basic decency.

Several days had been required in which to exhume the

airplane from its place of temporary interment and once more convert it to a usable tool. After he had removed the crusted snow that layered the wings and fuselage, the sun had made quick work of cleaning and drying the plane's skin. Then he had labored to shovel a path ahead of the plane's skis to the river's surface, and as he completed the chore, he once more felt the breathless exhaustion that forced him to rest more frequently than he wanted to.

With the heavy work done, he placed the bucket of black oil that had been drained several months earlier on the Yukon stove. While it slowly absorbed heat, he climbed the crude pole ladder to the cache, where, after barking his knee painfully, he found the plumber's stove and oil-stained tarp. After priming and lighting it, he carefully placed the hissing gas-fired device beneath the plane's nose before tenting both with the canvas.

Several hours passed, after which he removed the stove and tarp. This was followed by installation of the plane's battery, which, like its engine oil, had been stored inside. Finally, he poured the hot oil into the crankcase and pressed the starter button. The stone-nicked propeller turned through two reluctant revolutions before stopping, and the old man swore audibly. Still mumbling about batteries that lost their charge, he pulled the propeller through. On the third try the engine coughed, its blue exhaust quickly whisked away in the clean air.

The gray bitch raised her head slowly and pitched her ears in the direction of the faint sound, but after listening briefly, she looked away and resumed her nap.

The tiny clearing in which the old wolf lay was well packed with the wolves' tracks and beds. Only two main trails led to the place, and patches of brown moss and wood rot along with sodden clusters of dead grass were already evident where the sun lingered in the clearing's center during midday.

The four wolves had found the gut pile that the old man had left behind after butchering the moose he had taken for winter meat. It lay in the thawing snow almost five miles west of the cabin and at the base of a series of subridges that backed the higher one along the river. The wolves had fed on it until all that remained was a brown-stained oval of hard-packed snow. Finally, after the last visit, they had returned to the clearing with two of the hoofed lower legs, well fed by the standards of the late winter just past.

In the longer, warmer days that followed, had it not been for the almost daily regularity of the plane's roar as it departed and returned from somewhere downriver, the pack would have stayed in the vicinity of the opening. As it was, the gray bitch had grown restless first, and though the plane never passed directly over her, she came to anticipate its distance flattened sound during the middle hours of most mornings, and associated the sound with its source while the others did not. Finally, during an overcast afternoon and as if by previous agreement, the black, the female pup, and the single white female followed her as she struck out on an uphill course through the hazy gloom that blanketed the slope.

The old man's regular search for the wolves was limited only by bad weather and the dwindling supply of red gasoline that remained in the square tins and drums behind the cabin. The little plane's engine burned nearly ten gallons of it during each hour it flew, and to stretch what was left Tatum limited his time aloft to no more than sixty minutes per day.

Because of the decaying snow, he had reclaimed all of his traps and, as April ended, the snowmobile became virtually useless. Even the act of flying became increasingly hazardous as the river ice darkened and, glaciering, turned what remained of it to yellow-stained slush which dragged the plane's skis down and made taking off impossible in the short distance available.

The old man saw no wolves. He had cut the old line of thaw-elevated tracks left by the pack as it had ascended the drainage below Roosevelt and Hearst creeks during one of his first flights, but had learned nothing.

During the first week of May, the airplane had become his only means of transportation. When open gravel pans along the bar finally rendered his skis useless, he had replaced them with the big balloon-tired wheels and then waited impatiently for the sun to melt what snow still remained. Even these would eventually become useless, with rapidly rising water that would inevitably follow the soon-to-come final stages of breakup.

The wolves had left the valley of the Tatlanika via the crests of the high ridges that bordered it to the east. Though not by plan, their departure had been well camouflaged by dense alder and willow brush, which concealed the tracks they left in the remnant snow of the deep-cut and twisting gully they climbed. Once free of the steep slope, the black wolf had resumed his usual place at the head of the four-wolf pack, guiding it along the snow-free south-facing scree slopes. Then, after almost a week of slow and intermittent travel, the wolves took residence on a shelf-like gravel bench at the head of one of several tiny drainages that fed Fish Creek on the flats to the north. Here they rested.

The gray bitch once more felt the first feeble stirrings of life in her tightening belly as she lay flat on her side and with her legs outstretched on the warm, snow-free gravel. As she listened to the throaty gurglings of the tumbling creek below, she snapped at the gnats which already clustered along the edges of her ears and eyes.

Here on the high tundra, snow still lay in broad expanses that crumbled along their edges with softly audible sounds under the effects of the noon sun. Above the bench where the gray bitch lay, the mountains swept abruptly toward the pale-blue sky, their lower peaks still stark and white beneath a heavy layer of deep snow.

The old man had awakened early and, because he had slept little during the warm night, the result of overheating in his heavy blankets and a mild nausea, had gone directly to the airplane. After placing the stove and tarp and returning to the cabin, he had drunk warmed-over coffee as he waited for the engine to heat.

This would be his final hunt, for beyond his planned one hour of flight, only enough gasoline remained to take him to Fairbanks, where he would renew old acquaintances and tell hangar lies among his cronies. Even after the long solitude of the bitter winter, he did not really look forward to the trip, and was already planning his return to the cabin. During the previous day he had once more searched the countless western foothills of the range, and in doing so had reluctantly satisfied himself that no wolves were using the place that experience had taught him they favored. Today he would fly east.

The airplane droned smoothly as, in stages, it climbed the steepness of ridges behind the cabin, then, in level flight and under the old man's gentle urgings, began following the knife-edged lesser ridges that fanned away into the haze-filled distance.

The gray bitch trotted leisurely across the flat, open bench, pausing briefly to squat, urinate, and scratch before nuzzling her sleeping pup. The two then stood side by side, feeling the warmth in the building wind gusts generated by thermal updrafts as it ruffled the hair along their lean bellies. The two wolves were now identical both in size and coloration, and differed only in the slight limp that troubled the older wolf's gait as they trotted slowly along the lower edge of a dripping snow pan.

Somewhere higher on the slope, a ptarmigan, brown-speckled in its developing spring plumage, croaked discordantly, the sound at odds with the puny squeaking of a circling eagle as the bird soared on still wings above the rougher air.

Dropping lower, the old man also felt the rising strength in the sharp gusts that rocked the little airplane's wings. He did not like turbulent air and, as the plane bucked heavily during its swift passage over yet another of the sharp ridge crests, he began to think about calling off the search and returning to the stability of the gravel bar near the cabin. It was at this precise moment that he spotted the four undulating track lines which bridged a wide patch of snow before ending abruptly in the shale and rock debris beyond.

At first, the engine sound was only a faint disturbance that was felt rather than heard by the gray bitch. The wind hid most of it, obscuring its source, and she swung her head in half-interested efforts to pin it down. If the pup at her side heard the faint reverberations she gave no sign as, grunting contentedly, she curled up once more in the brilliant sun to resume her intermittent day-long nap.

The airplane circled lower under reduced power, its wings rocking sluggishly in the decreased airspeed at which it now flew. The old man executed two low passes over the tracks, the second made only to assure him that what his eyes had seen during the first was true. As he fed power to the engine, he was already anticipating what he would find on the far side of the crest, and the hunt was on.

Panting lightly, the old bitch stood, then trotted quickly back to her sleeping mate, who dozed on the far side of the bench. His ears traced her approach and, stretching his powerful dun-gray forelegs, he greeted her with his slowly wagging tail as she drew near.

Tatum's left hand slid the knoblike throttle handle rearward as his right simultaneously placed light back pressure on the worn smoothness of the control stick. He gazed intently through the blur made by the spinning propeller, and his eyes smarted as he watched the snow-mottled ridge slip beneath the plane's belly to course upward behind him. More tracks appeared briefly, then flickered to nothingness, but not before betraying the direction in which their makers had traveled.

Studying the sporadic sign, the old man clenched his fist as, once more, the tingling cramp spread from his shoulder into his arm, but he ignored it just as he ignored the moving hands on the old pocket watch he had taped to the instrument panel ahead of him. During his younger days he would have scanned the timepiece and, knowing how much fuel the engine burned during a given unit of time, checked what it told him against the wing-root fuel gauge to the right of his head. Had he done so now, he would have learned that the tanks, which rode in the plane's wings, were nearly empty.

The sudden wash of sound that finally overrode those made by the wind caused the gray bitch to flatten herself as it simultaneously roused her mate from sleep. It came from above and behind the shelf-like perimeter of the bench, and even as she watched in stunned immobility, the plane loomed large in her vision, its shadow momentarily blotting out the sun as it passed less than a hundred feet overhead.

The old man saw only two wolves. One was gray, the other white, and both were curled as if asleep on the exposed flat place that had flashed beneath the plane before being absorbed by the seventy-miles-per-hour speed at which it traveled. Many hours of wolf hunting smothered the impulse to add full power and return to the scene as quickly as possible. Instead, he continued his gentle climb until well below the wolves. Here he started a slow turn to the west while checking the semiautomatic shotgun's breech for the live shell he knew was there.

The gray bitch began her escape long before the plane disappeared from sight, lost in the haze that softened the

contours of the lower hills. It is doubtful that the black wolf
followed out of the same fear that she felt, for he had little
experience in the matter of airplanes.

Both wolves trotted rapidly to the lowermost edge of the
shelf-like bench, glanced over their shoulders at the resident
bitch and the pup, then ghosted from sight into the fur-
rowed steepness of the willow-carpeted slope which ended
abruptly in the brush of the creekbed.

Righting the plane after being jammed by a strong gust,
the old man continued to climb the slope. To approach from
this direction was dangerous, a fact discovered by others
when, during the last few seconds, their planes could not
outclimb the terrain ahead. Yet, time for the old man had
become precious, and the fact that he had done it many
times in the past numbed the quick pangs of caution.

Flying almost level toward the slope, he relocated the tiny
bench over the plane's cowl. Then, cautiously adding power,
he moved his left hand to the floor-mounted lever that de-
ployed the plane's wing flaps, which, in turn, acted as brakes,
allowing the plane to be flown at its slowest speed. As he
felt the ratcheting lever engage and the plane decelerate, he
was once more aware of the vague tightness in his chest and
the cramping dullness of pain that grew in his left arm.

The white female stood her ground, transfixed by the
seemingly stationary object that now approached her head-
on. She failed to perceive its growth in size as she listened to
its hypnotic hissing, chuckling sound. Though the pup also
heard the approaching plane, she still lay nearby, only curious and as yet unaware of the source from which the noise
came.

The old man's reflexes, despite the almost seventy years
during which they had served his needs, played a major part
in the events that followed. Adjusting the plane's power one
last time, he pushed the left side window rearward. Then,
gripping the control stick between his knees, he slid the

shotgun muzzle-first into the cold slipstream. Finally, blinking away the tears which blurred his vision, he slipped the safety catch on the gun.

The pup, rising to her feet as the plane's sound grew rapidly in her ears, was slammed sideways as six of the heavy buckshot pellets penetrated her chest before angling downward to explode in the loose gravel beneath her. The muffled report of the heavy gun caused the white bitch's fast trot to become a loping run. She chose the natural direction of flight away from the plane, and the decision sealed her doom. Tatum's second shot followed less than a second behind the first, shattering her hindquarters and rolling her end over end, her scream of pain drowned in the howl of the engine as the plane leaped away under full power.

The old man held his breath, resisting the overwhelming desire to jerk back on the stick and bring the plane's nose skyward. To do so would have been to stall it by increasing the angle at which the wings bit at the air, making them unable to support the plane's weight and causing it to nose down into the ground which rushed by, scant feet below.

Finally, the big wheels almost touching the moss, the plane shot over the crest of the ridge in a steep climb, and the deep vault of blue sky replaced the racing tapestry of snow patches and tundra that had filled its windshield only moments before.

The black wolf paused as the muted explosion merged and reached his ears, and mindless of his mate's continued flight ahead of him in the deep-cut gully, he climbed the creek's overhanging bank to emerge from the short willows that crowned it. Here he studied the steep slope he had just ascended. He stood on the open mossy softness of the barren hillside, his flattened ears and lolling tongue telling of the exertion he had expended in the creekbed.

Turning the plane once more, the old man recrossed the

ridge above the bench. As he did, he spotted the big black where he stood motionless in a patch of afternoon sun farther down the valley. Once more he slid the throttle post to the rear, feeling it come against the stop, and with the engine running at idle speed, he prepared to shoot once more.

The black wolf continued to stand motionless as he watched the approaching plane, and as the distance shortened rapidly, the old man gasped as he realized the sheer size of the pack leader. Fragmentary visions of huge tracks near a torn snowmobile and in the snow near the Tatlanika kill below the cabin flickered to life, then slipped from conscious thought as he once more readied the shotgun and fought the tears that came quickly in the cold air that pummeled his bearded face before spreading backward across his cheeks.

The big wolf turned to flee just as the old man's cold-numbed finger closed on the gun's trigger, and the explosion reached his ears during the tumbling fall that ended in a confusion of icy creek water. The black felt no pain as he regained his feet, only the spreading numbness in his hips, and the unfamiliar sensation made running somehow difficult and frustrating in its inefficiency.

The old man knew that he had missed even as the heavy shotgun bucked unnoticed at his shoulder, and he cursed his carelessness in helpless rage while slamming his hand against the instrument panel. Then, turning the craft steeply, he began a final pass up the meandering gully with its ribbon of tumbling white water. As he did, his eyes swept the now motionless needle in the fuel gauge.

Looking ahead once more, the fact that the plane was already critically short of fuel making a cold knot in his stomach, the old man knew there was little hope of seeing the black wolf a second time. Then, cursing again, he felt the throat-constricting pain that tightened his chest and shut off his breathing. He found that he could not move his arms, and the need to once more add power to clear the ridge ahead suddenly seemed unimportant. In his blurred and darkening vision, he watched abstractedly as the soft carpet of green-brown tundra reached up to claim him.

Jake Tatum was mercifully unaware of the plane's impact as it struck the slope at a steep angle just below its upper edge. Neither did he feel the ripping, tearing forces that stripped one of the plane's wings from its fuselage moments before the engine was driven backward into his lap and chest. Perhaps most merciful of all was the fact that he never knew of the searing incineration that blossomed and consumed the fragile plane in less than a minute after the escaping fuel vapor contacted open electric leads around the torn engine. Jake Tatum's heart had stopped and he was dead before all of these things occurred.

The small gray bitch slipped unnoticed over the ridge well above the place where the plane came to rest, a dark speck moving over a vast snowslide. She had heard the insignificant sounds it made as it destroyed itself behind her, just as she had heard the explosion of the shotgun. Then the windswept silence of her own world had returned as she reached the ridge crest and was gone.

Long walls of deep shadow washed the valleys as she trotted slowly eastward. Still limping badly, the course she chose did not, as always, come from a conscious decision, nor was it influenced by the huge black wolf that had trailed her and finally caught up, his hip matted with the drying blood of his wound.

The pair walked in the orange light of the spring evening, once more traversing the high ridges as their long shadows reached outward behind them to mock their trotting gait. The gray bitch sensed the events that had occurred as a vague uneasiness rather than as the stunning fear that had consumed her near the kill on the Tatlanika, for she had been well away from the carnage on the gravel bench. The black had not.

The single lead pellet had passed through the heavy muscles of his upper hind leg, numbing it and staining the loose snow in the creekbed scarlet as he fought to catch his mate. Before doing so, shock had turned to cramping pain, and though the dark hair on his hip stanched the bleeding, he limped badly. No bone had been broken, and the wound would heal.

With her new pregnancy the old bitch's body was once more disproportionate in its depth, and as she trotted ahead of the black wolf, the warm living scents of the new spring washed her gray muzzle. It was perhaps because of these things that she carried her tail higher than usual. Then, following their shadows, the two wolves disappeared into the darkness of the deep valley that concealed St. George Creek. Another summer was close at hand.